Building Claude Skills

Turn repeatable work into reusable Claude Skills

Pietro Montaldo

<packt>

Building Claude Skills

Portfolio Director: Pavan Ramchandani

Portfolio Manager: Mohd Riyan Khan

Program Manager: Divij Kotian

Content Engineer: Mohd Hammad

Technical Editor: Vidhisha Patidar

Indexer: Manju Arasan

Production Designer: Jyoti Kadam

Growth Lead: Prajwal S

First published: August 2026

Production reference: 2120826

Published by Packt Publishing Ltd.
Grosvenor House
11 St Paul's Square
Birmingham
B3 1RB, UK.

ISBN 978-1-80849-285-3

www.packtpub.com

Contributors

About the author

Pietro Montaldo is the founder of NotLinear, an AI education company teaching non-technical operators how to run AI at work. He scaled a software company from $0 to $1M in 12 months, then co-founded NForce, an AI development agency with clients on four continents. He has trained 5,000+ operators from companies such as Gartner, TikTok, Warner Bros., J&J, and PayPal, and his content reaches 500,000+ professionals each month. Before founding NotLinear, Pietro studied finance at Università Bocconi and worked at Project A, a top-tier VC firm. He runs live training sessions, including his bestselling Maven course, *Claude for Non-Technical Operators*, and writes the newsletter *Building with AI for Non-Techies*. Originally from Italy, he now lives in Barcelona, Spain.

Table of Contents

Preface

Claude can do almost anything you describe in words: draft a proposal, prepare an invoice, build a presentation, or write a follow-up email after a call. But if you ask for any of this without giving Claude any guidance on how you like the work done, you get a generic result. That result is simply the most likely answer to your request, and it is unlikely to sound like you, follow your formatting rules, or meet the standard you would be comfortable sharing with a colleague or a customer.

A *skill* solves this problem. It is a reusable, saved set of instructions that teaches Claude how you want a specific, recurring task completed, in the same way that you would onboard a new team member by giving them your branding, your tone of voice, your examples of good work, and the steps you expect them to follow. Once a skill is saved, Claude loads it automatically whenever a request matches the task it covers across **Claude Chat**, **Claude Cowork**, and **Claude Code**, so the process, and not just a single answer, becomes something you can rely on and reuse.

This book is a practical, hands-on guide to building, refining, testing, and extending skills. It starts by placing skills within the wider Claude ecosystem, alongside **projects**, **connectors**, and **custom instructions**, and by examining exactly what a skill contains. It then walks through five different methods for creating a skill, the design principles that keep a skill focused and efficient, the testing methods that make a skill dependable enough for important, customer-facing work, and finally how skills can be extended with connectors to external tools and with subagents that take on heavier, more repetitive work outside the main conversation.

Throughout the book, the recurring idea is that a skill does not replace your judgment, your creativity, or your voice. It removes the repetitive parts of a task that do not require those things, so that Claude becomes an instrument that makes you faster and more effective at the work you already understand, while you remain the one directing where that work goes.

Who this book is for

This book is written for professionals who already use Claude for day-to-day tasks and want to move from one-off prompting to dependable, reusable workflows. It is particularly useful for non-technical professionals in roles such as sales, marketing, operations, and business leadership, who repeatedly perform the same kind of task, such as drafting follow-up emails, preparing for meetings, generating reports or invoices, or working with tools such as a **CRM**, **Asana**, or **Stripe**, and who want to teach Claude to handle more of that repeated work reliably.

No programming background is required to follow this book. A **Claude account** with access to the **Customize** and **Skills** sections is the only strict requirement. Claude Cowork is needed to follow the more advanced examples in later chapters that involve local file access, browser control, scheduled automation, and subagents, but most of the book's methods can also be followed in Claude Chat.

What this book covers

Chapter 1, Understanding Claude Skills and Their Place in the Ecosystem, maps Claude as an ecosystem of four layers, interfaces, workspaces, native capabilities, and extensions, and places **skills** within the extensions layer. It defines what a *skill* is, examines its anatomy (the required SKILL.md file and the optional references, assets, and scripts), explains the standalone .md and packaged .zip or .skill file formats, distinguishes skills from projects, connectors, and custom instructions, and introduces the four types of skills: **Anthropic-generated**, **custom**, **organization-provisioned**, and **partner skills**.

Chapter 2, Five Methods for Creating Claude Skills, covers the five ways a skill can be created: using **Anthropic's built-in Skill Creator**; completing a task successfully and then converting it into a skill, which is the method recommended most strongly for everyday use; migrating an existing **Custom GPT**, **Gemini Gem**, or **Project** from another AI platform; planning and designing a complex skill in a document before it is built; and importing and adapting a skill that someone else has already created.

Chapter 3, Designing Focused and Efficient Skills, sets out the design principles that keep a skill dependable: giving it a single job, starting with a simple version and improving it through repeated use, keeping human-in-the-loop checkpoints where your judgement or approval still matters, using examples to define what a successful output looks like, respecting **Anthropic's 500-line guideline** for a skill's core instructions, splitting an overloaded skill into several focused ones, moving supporting material into reference files, and choosing which recurring tasks are worth turning into a skill in the first place.

Chapter 4, Testing, Maintaining, and Sharing Skills, introduces a **quality loop** built on three testing methods: **evals**, which check a skill against objective requirements; **A/B testing**, which compares two versions of a skill through a blind judgement; and **trigger testing**, which checks whether a skill activates at the right moment. It also covers the difference between **hosted** and **local skills**, the four routes for sharing a skill with a team or an organization, and closes with a detailed walk-through of a sophisticated pre-call briefing skill that coordinates several connected tools to produce more than one polished output.

Chapter 5, Extending Skills with Connectors and Subagents, explains how connectors give Claude access to external systems such as a CRM, Asana, Stripe, or a calendar, and introduces the **Model Context Protocol (MCP)** that underpins them, along with the five levels through which

Claude can reach an external tool, from native connectors through to browser use and computer control. It then shows how skills are built on top of connectors, and introduces **subagents** as a way to delegate repeated, context-heavy work to separate copies of Claude, including how skills and subagents complement each other and the limitations of subagents.

To get the most out of this book

You will get the most from this book if you have a Claude account with access to the **Customize** and **Skills** sections, and if you follow the examples in your own account as you read, rather than reading about them only in theory. The following will help you follow every example in the book:

- A Claude account with access to the **Customize** and **Skills** sections.
- Access to Claude Cowork, where available to you. Cowork can be used on desktop, web, and mobile, although availability may vary according to your account plan and organizational settings. Most examples can be followed in Claude Chat, but scheduled automation and subagent workflows require Cowork. Tasks that access local files or control a browser or computer through Cowork may also require the Claude Desktop app to be installed and open.
- Access to Claude in Chrome, used in the chapters that demonstrate browser-based tasks, such as migrating a workflow from another AI platform.
- Optionally, accounts for any connected services you want to try alongside the book's examples, such as Gmail, Google Calendar, a call-recording tool, a CRM such as HubSpot, Asana, or Stripe. These services support specific demonstrations in the book, but they are not required to understand or apply the underlying methods.

No programming knowledge is required anywhere in this book. Every method, from creating a skill to testing it and extending it with connectors and subagents, is driven by ordinary requests you type into Claude.

Access to Claude Cowork, specific Cowork capabilities, and connectors can depend on your account type, the device or interface you are using, and the policies your organization applies. If a feature described in the book is not available to you, the surrounding explanation still applies, and most of the book's core methods can be followed in Claude Chat alone.

Download the sample skill bundle

This book includes a downloadable bundle containing the skills developed by the author. You can use these skills to experiment with the examples and as a practical starting point for your own work. Modify and extend them, or create your own variations as you progress through the chapters.

Get the skill bundle

If you bought the book directly from Packt:

1. Go to `packtpub.com`
2. Click your **profile picture** and select **Your Orders**
3. Find this book and click **Download Code**

If you bought this book from Amazon or any other channel partner:

1. Go to `packtpub.com/unlock` or scan the following QR code:

2. Search for this book
3. Sign up or log in to your free Packt account
4. Upload your proof of purchase and download the skill bundle locally

Usage note: You're free to use and modify these skills in your own work, including inside your company. You may not redistribute or resell them.

Download the color images

Your purchase includes a color, DRM-free PDF copy of this book, ideal for viewing color images, screenshots, and diagrams. Refer to *Free benefits with your book* section at the end of the *Preface* to unlock your PDF copy.

Conventions used

A number of conventions are used throughout this book. Prompts you can type directly into **Claude** are shown on their own, appearing different from the surrounding text, so that you can easily identify and reuse them, for example:

```
Based on the content of this conversation, please generate a skill to follow up on
any sales conversation which I have.
```

Interface elements you select, such as menu items and buttons, are shown in *bold*, for example, select **Save skill** or open **Customize**. Numbered figures throughout the book show screenshots of the **Claude interface** being discussed, and are referenced in the text, for example, *Figure 1.1*.

Get in touch

Feedback from our readers is always welcome.

General feedback: If you have questions about any aspect of this book, or have any general feedback, please email us at customercare@packt.com and mention the book's title in the subject of your message.

Errata: Although we have taken every care to ensure the accuracy of our content, mistakes do happen. If you have found a mistake in this book, we would be grateful if you reported this to us. Please visit `http://www.packt.com/submit-errata`, click **Submit Errata**, and fill in the form.

Piracy: If you come across any illegal copies of our works in any form on the internet, we would be grateful if you would provide us with the location address or website name. Please contact us at copyright@packt.com with a link to the material.

If you are interested in becoming an author: If there is a topic that you have expertise in and you are interested in either writing or contributing to a book, please visit `http://authors.packt.com/`.

Free benefits with your book

This book includes free benefits designed to support your learning and help you apply what you learn effectively. Activate them now for instant access (see the *How to unlock* section for instructions).

Here's a quick overview of what you can instantly unlock with your purchase:

Complete Code Bundle

Download the full source code for this book's examples and projects.

DRM-Free PDF Version

Download DRM-free PDF and ePub copies of this book.

7-Day Packt Library Access

Get 7-day unlimited access to 8,000+ books and videos. No credit card required.

Available for first-time Packt+ trial users only.

Next-Gen Reader Access

Read this book on Packt Reader with progress sync, dark mode and note-taking.

How to unlock

Scan the QR code (or go to `packtpub.com/unlock`). Search for this book by name, confirm the edition, and then follow the steps on the page.

UNLOCK NOW

Note: Have your invoice handy. Purchases made directly from the Packt website don't require an invoice.

Share your thoughts

Once you've read *Building Claude Skills,* we'd love to hear your thoughts! Scan the QR code below to go straight to the Amazon review page for this book and share your feedback.

`https://packt.link/r/1808492854`

Your review is *important* to us and the tech community and will help us make sure we're delivering excellent quality content.

1

Understanding Claude Skills and Their Place in the Ecosystem

Before we begin building skills, we need a clear understanding of the key tools and terminology used across the **Claude ecosystem**. This chapter focuses on skills, so it does not explain every Claude capability in detail. Other features are introduced only where they help us understand where skills sit and how they interact with the rest of the ecosystem.

We start with a snapshot of Claude as an ecosystem rather than a single chatbot. From there, we define what a *skill* is, examine what exists inside one, and look at the two formats in which a skill can be shared. We then distinguish skills from **projects**, **connectors**, and **custom instructions**, review the interfaces in which skills can run, and cover the four types of skills that are available. By the end of the chapter, you will understand what a skill is, what it contains, and where it belongs in the wider ecosystem. This foundation will prepare you to create your own skills in the chapters that follow.

In this chapter, we will cover the following topics:

- Mapping the Claude ecosystem
- Understanding what a skill is
- Examining the anatomy of a skill
- Understanding skill file formats and sharing methods
- Comparing skills with projects
- Choosing the right interface for a skill
- Distinguishing skills from related Claude capabilities
- Understanding the four types of skills
- Finding existing skills

NOTE

Download the sample skill bundle and the PDF version of this book

Your purchase includes a DRM-free PDF copy of this book, the sample skill bundle, and a range of exclusive benefits. To unlock everything, follow the Free benefits with your book section in the Preface.

Technical requirements

To follow the interface examples in this chapter, you will need the following:

- A Claude account with access to **Claude Chat**
- Access to the **Customize** and Skills **sections** of the interface
- **Claude Cowork**, where it is available to you

Access to **Claude Cowork** can depend on your account type and on the policies applied by your organization. Most standard work can still be completed through Claude Chat, but some capabilities discussed in this chapter, including access to local files and scheduled automation, are only available in Cowork.

Mapping the Claude ecosystem

Before placing skills within Claude, we need a shared understanding of the tools and terminology used across the ecosystem. Claude is not a single chatbot; it is an *ecosystem* that can be divided into four layers:

- **Interfaces**
- **Workspaces**
- **Native capabilities**
- **Extensions**

Each layer answers a different question. **Interfaces** determine which Claude product you are working with. **Workspaces** determine how your work is organized. **Native capabilities** describe what Claude can do by design. **Extensions** add your own knowledge and connections on top of the system that Anthropic has already built. Skills belong to the extensions layer, which is the part of the ecosystem this book focuses on most closely.

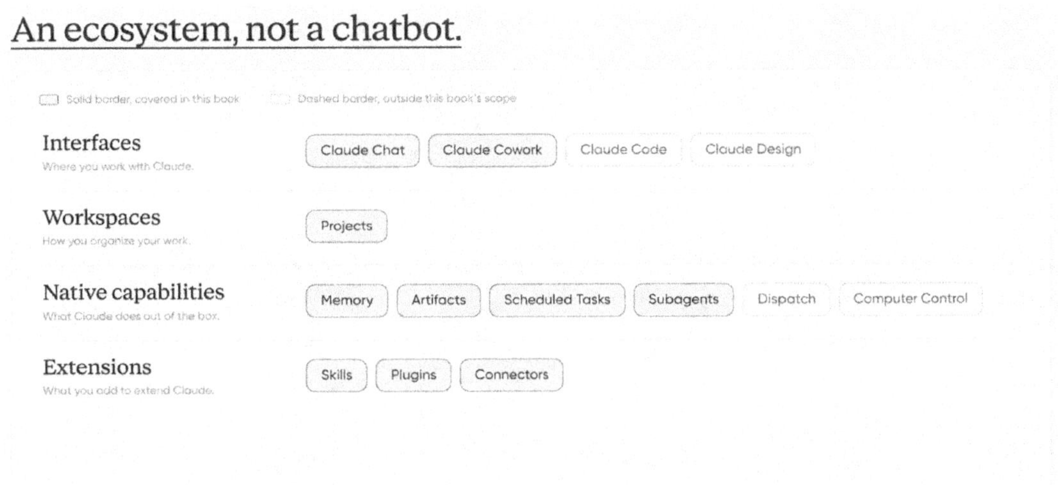

Figure 1.1: The four layers of the Claude ecosystem

Interfaces

The first layer contains the interfaces, which are the products you choose according to the task you want to complete. The interface most people are familiar with is Claude Chat, a back-and-forth conversation in which you ask a question and Claude answers.

The second interface is Claude Cowork, which supports more ambitious work involving planning, external tools, browser activity, local files, or longer-running tasks. Cowork can be understood as *Claude Code* for non-technical people, because it provides a more powerful interface for work that goes beyond an ordinary chat.

Claude also provides two further interfaces. **Claude Code** is used to ship and edit software, while **Claude Design** is used for design-related work. The decision at this layer is straightforward: you need to pick the right Claude product for the specific task you want to do.

Because the two interfaces most people use day to day, Claude Chat and Claude Cowork, determine which skills can run where, it is worth setting out their differences early. *Figure 1.2* compares what each interface can do.

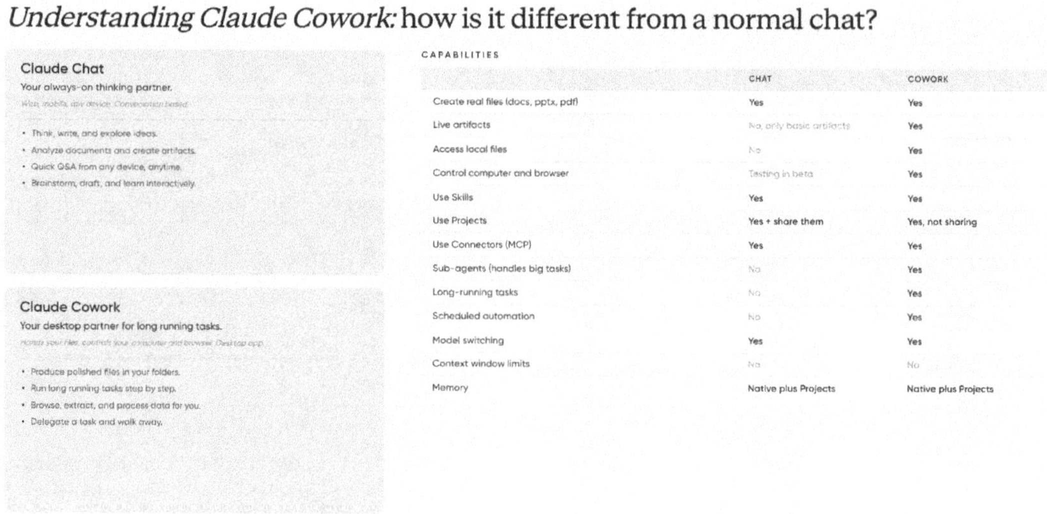

	CHAT	COWORK
Create real files (docs, pptx, pdf)	Yes	Yes
Live artifacts	No, only basic artifacts	Yes
Access local files	No	Yes
Control computer and browser	Testing in beta	Yes
Use Skills	Yes	Yes
Use Projects	Yes + share them	Yes, not sharing
Use Connectors (MCP)	Yes	Yes
Sub-agents (handles big tasks)	No	Yes
Long-running tasks	No	Yes
Scheduled automation	No	Yes
Model switching	Yes	Yes
Context window limits	No	No
Memory	Native plus Projects	Native plus Projects

Figure 1.2: A comparison of Claude Chat and Claude Cowork

Workspaces

The second layer is **workspaces**, which determine how you organize your work inside Claude. A workspace can be imagined as a folder inside Claude, because it lets you organize the information Claude reads and writes while working on a particular topic or customer. In practice, this layer is represented through **projects**. We will compare projects with skills in more detail later in the chapter.

Native capabilities

The third layer contains Claude's **native capabilities**, which are the things Claude is designed to do out of the box, without you adding them separately. **Memory** allows Claude to remember information, including details about you. **Artifacts** are shareable assets that Claude creates, such as PDFs, dashboards, and presentations; in the interface, an artifact generally appears on the right side of the conversation. **Scheduled tasks** allow work to happen without you needing to trigger it manually. **Subagents** determine how Claude organizes work when a task involves multiple repeated activities and requires a team of agents rather than a single one. The ecosystem also includes capabilities such as **computer control** and **Dispatch**, which sit alongside the other native capabilities but are outside the central scope of this chapter.

Extensions

The fourth layer is **extensions**, which is the area this book focuses on most closely. *Extensions* are what you add to extend Claude: they build on top of the interfaces, workspaces, and native capabilities that Anthropic has developed, and they extend the ecosystem with your own knowledge. The extension layer contains **skills**, **plugins**, and **connectors**.

Skills are the central extension in this book because they allow you to teach Claude how to perform tasks according to your preferred process and requirements. Consider creating a presentation. The way one person creates a presentation is different from the way another person does, because they follow different rules, work in different fields, and speak to different audiences. If you instruct Claude to create a presentation through one of your skills, that skill captures the way you want the presentation created, so the output is more closely aligned with your requirements. Everything else in this layer, and in the other three layers, remains a supporting topic; what matters is knowing where these pieces sit and how skills interact with each one.

Understanding what a skill is

A *skill* is, technically, a reusable set of instructions that teaches Claude how you like a specific task done. If you ask Claude to create something without a skill, for example, a report for your manager, a presentation for an investor, or a sales proposal for a potential customer, and you do not teach it how you want the work done, you will get a generic result. That generic result is simply the most likely response to the request, and it is unlikely to meet your expectations.

Think of it like onboarding a new team member. If you ask an intern to prepare a presentation or a proposal without giving them your branding, the tone you want, or your formatting rules, the result will probably not satisfy you, and you will not be comfortable sharing it externally. A skill solves the same problem for Claude. It acts like a *standard operating procedure* that teaches Claude how to complete a specific task, helping it produce work that is more consistent with your requirements and suitable for everyday or external use. This is why skills are so powerful: they teach Claude how to perform a specific task rather than leaving it to guess the process from a general request.

Examining the anatomy of a skill

A skill is made up of four parts, but only one of them is required. The single required part is the `SKILL.md` file; the other three parts, references, assets, and scripts, are optional. When Claude helps you create a skill, it can organize the information you provide into these components. You should still understand the structure so that you can review and maintain the skill as it develops. What matters is knowing what a skill can contain and ***remembering that the SKILL.md file is always required.***

The four parts map directly onto a skill folder. The following structure reproduces that layout, with the required file at the top and the three optional directories beneath it:

```
your-skill-name/
├── SKILL.md (required) The metadata and core instructions
├── references/ (optional) Extra documents, style guides, and examples
├── assets/ (optional) Templates, fonts, images, and icons
└── scripts/ (optional) Code that Claude can run
```

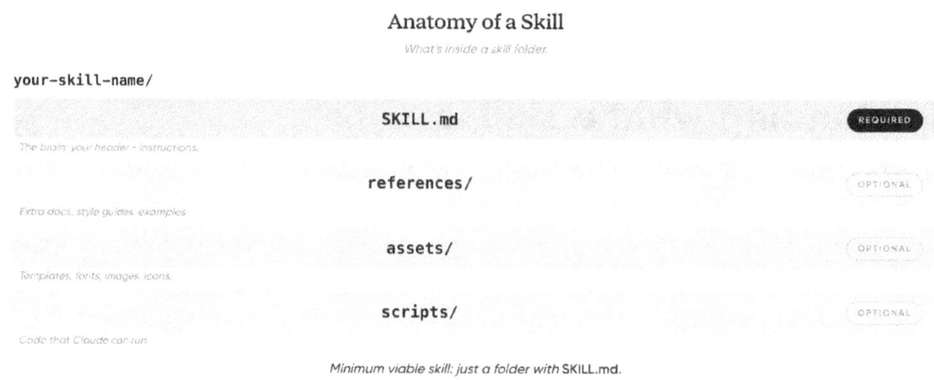

Figure 1.3: The required and optional components of a skill

The SKILL.md file

You cannot have a skill without a `SKILL.md` file, which is a document written in the **Markdown** format. Markdown is a lightweight plain-text format that uses simple characters to structure headings, lists, links, and other content. The `SKILL.md` file contains the information Claude needs to perform the task. This file is the core of the skill; it is a written set of instructions describing how Claude should complete that specific task.

References

References might be examples of successful past work, such as previous presentations or invoices, or your formatting rules and style guides. They help Claude understand what good output looks like.

Assets

Assets are files used in the output or during execution, such as your logo, images, icons, or templates.

Scripts

Scripts are snippets of code that Claude can run when a task requires a calculation or another programmatic step, such as calculating taxes or referencing something external. Claude can generate the scripts required by the workflow, so you do not necessarily need to write the code yourself.

References, assets, and scripts are all optional. You can have a skill with only a `SKILL.md` file, or a skill that also carries all three. When you open the **Skills** section in Claude, you will see examples of both simple and complex skills. A simple skill, such as one that generates a follow-up after a sales meeting, might contain only its `SKILL.md` file. A more complex skill, such as one that generates invoices, can include assets (for example, a logo), references (past invoices, so Claude knows what good looks like), and scripts (code for calculations). The following figure shows the Claude interface with a skill that includes all four components: `SKILL.md`, assets, references, and scripts.

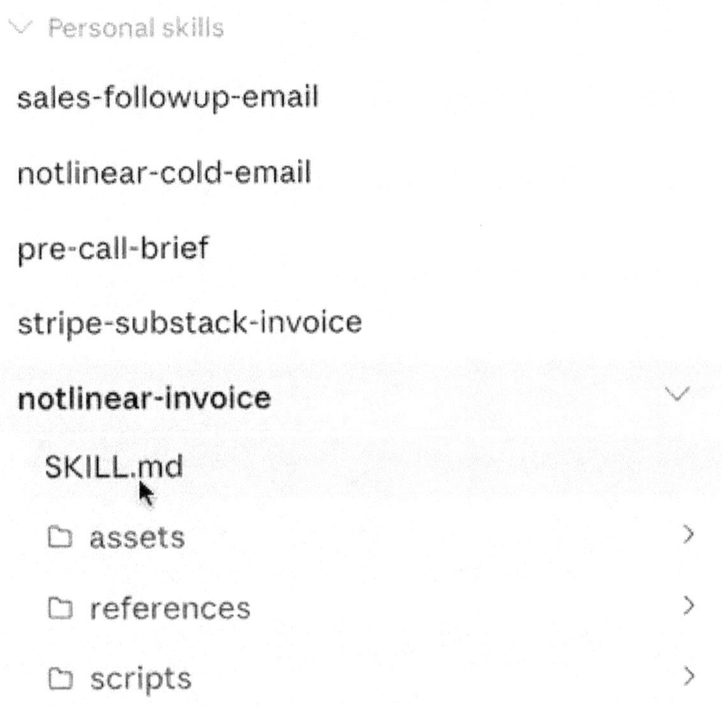

Figure 1.4: The notlinear-invoice skill expanded to show SKILL.md and its supporting folders

Understanding skill file formats and sharing methods

A skill can be shared in two forms. The first is a standalone `.md` file containing the core instructions. The second is a packaged archive containing `SKILL.md` together with any supporting files, such as references, assets, and scripts. Packaged skills commonly use the `.skill` extension, although Claude also accepts a `.zip` archive containing the same files.

To upload a skill, open the **Skills** section, select **Create skill**, and choose **Upload a skill**. As shown in *Figure 1.5*, a standalone `.md` file must contain the skill name and description formatted in YAML, while a `.zip` or `.skill` package must include a `SKILL.md` file.

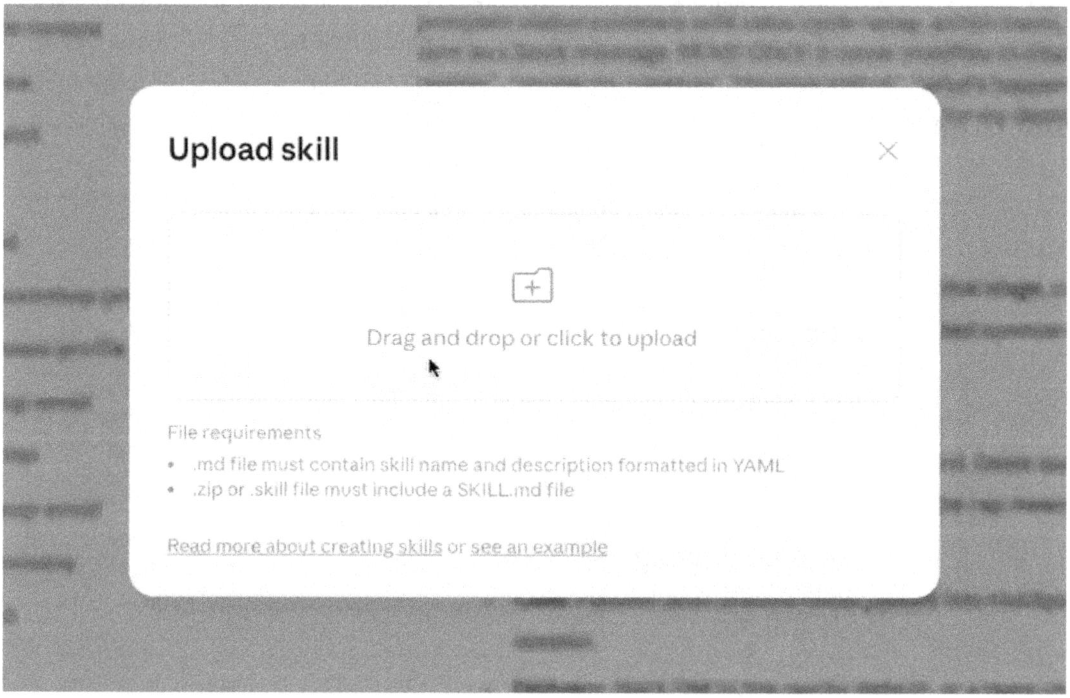

Figure 1.5: File requirements for uploading standalone and packaged skills

At this point, we have the technical foundation of a skill: why you use one, what exists inside it, and which formats Claude accepts. The next distinction is equally important: *understanding when the information belongs in a skill and when it belongs in a project.*

Comparing skills with projects

One of the most common questions is whether a particular body of work should be organized as a project or as a skill. For example, if you have a customer, should you create a project for them or a skill? If you want to generate a presentation, should you use a skill, or create a project that holds all your past presentations? Projects and skills serve different purposes, and the distinction comes down to *what* versus *how*.

A project is the *what*. It contains all the context and information about your work. For a client, a project would include all past engagements, contracts, profiles, and any files related to that client or workflow. You can think of a project as a folder, similar to Google Drive or Microsoft 365, where you store everything relevant to a specific workflow or client, so that it is easy to find what you need when you work on that topic.

A skill is the *how*. It defines the expertise for completing a specific task: best practices, formatting rules, and processes. For instance, if you have three clients, you would have one project for each, and each project would hold the context for that client. You might then have a single skill for generating a proposal or a presentation, which you can apply to client A, client B, or client C. The skill provides the process, while the project provides the context.

In other words, a project stores knowledge that Claude can reference, while a skill defines a process that Claude can execute. These are not alternatives. Projects and skills can be used together effectively: store all the context in projects, and use skills across those projects as needed. Combining context with expertise produces a professional, personalized output.

Another key difference is that skills are portable. When we say portable, we mean you can call a skill in any conversation you like; you do not have to start the conversation in a specific section of Claude. For example, if you are working in a project called Client A, you can still call any skill in your account at any point. Imagine a conversation that begins as preparation for a webinar and develops into material that would make a good LinkedIn post. If your account includes a skill for creating LinkedIn posts, you can invoke it at that point and use the context of the conversation. Skills can be called across all interfaces, including **Chat**, **Cowork**, and **Code**, and at any point in any conversation.

Projects work differently. To access the context stored in a project, including all the files you have placed there, you must start the conversation within that project. A conversation started elsewhere will not have access to that material. So a skill is portable across conversations by design, while a project's context is only available when the conversation begins inside that project. Having a clear understanding of how skills and projects are positioned relative to each other will help you use the Claude ecosystem more effectively.

Choosing the right interface for a skill

The next distinction concerns the difference between using a skill in **Cowork** versus using it in a standard **chat**, and what you should be careful about when choosing where to run your skills.

Using skills in Chat and Cowork

You can teach a skill to do almost anything you can describe in text. Some skills, however, involve more complex operations: browsing to LinkedIn on your behalf and extracting information about a person, using subagents, running a `script`, or accessing local files. A skill can only use one of these capabilities if the current interface supports it. When you use a skill that requires advanced features such as local file access, browser control, running scripts, or executing long-running tasks, those capabilities are only available in Claude Cowork or Claude Code. If you try to use such a skill in Claude Chat, the skill will still trigger, but it will not be able to perform the intended task, because Chat does not support those features. **This is crucial**: if you build a skill for Cowork or Code and then call it in Chat, you will not get the expected results.

Claude Chat is the standard conversational interface. Claude Cowork is a more powerful interface with additional features and can be understood as the non-technical equivalent of Claude Code. If you want to follow the advanced examples, you should have Claude Cowork. You can switch between Chat and Cowork using the **interface selector**. The capability comparison in *Figure 1.2* summarizes which features are available in each interface.

If your organization does not provide access to Cowork, you will face some limitations. Most standard tasks can still be completed in Claude Chat, but features such as accessing local folders or scheduling automations are available only in Cowork. Access may also be controlled through organization-wide policies. **Understanding which features are available in each interface is therefore especially important** when Cowork access is restricted, because the interface must support the capabilities required by the skill for the full workflow to run.

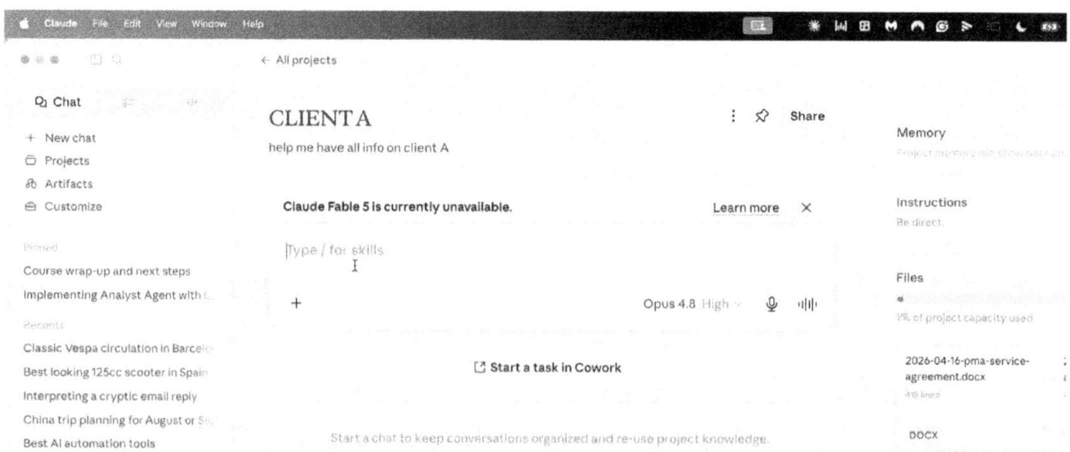

Figure 1.6: The Claude Chat interface

The Claude Chat interface is where you type prompts and hold a back-and-forth conversation. The Claude Cowork interface, by contrast, provides access to more advanced features, including long-running tasks and browser control.

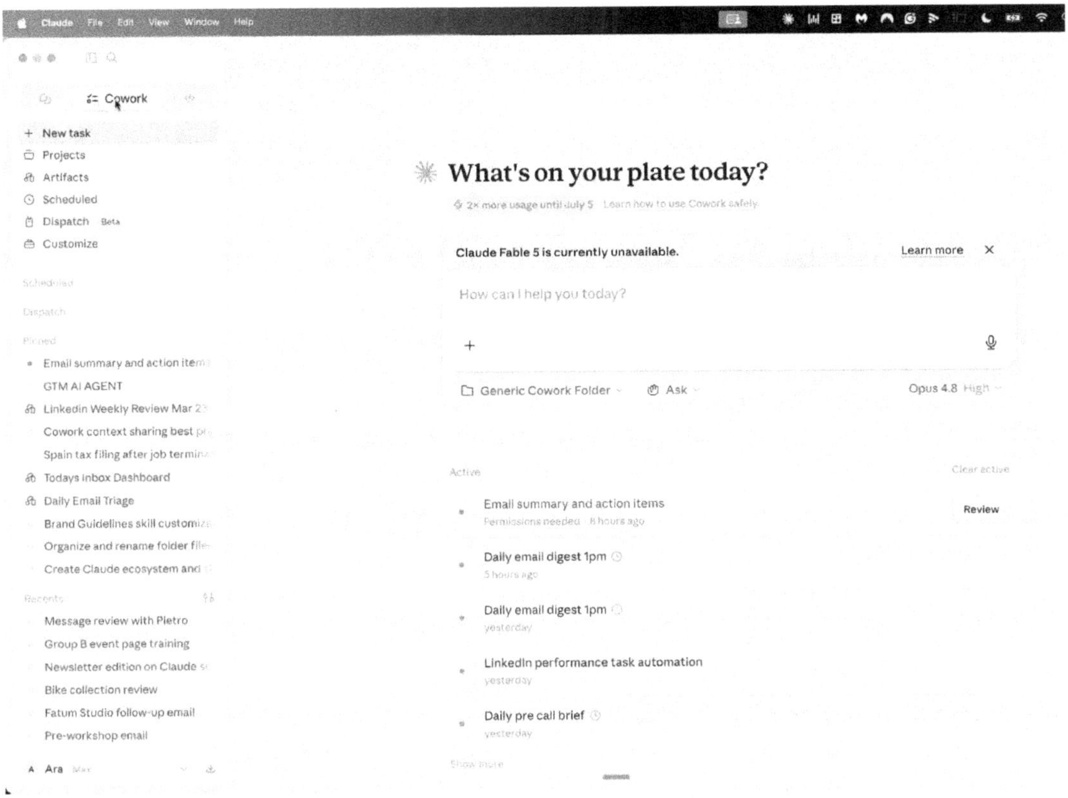

Figure 1.7: The Claude Cowork interface

Distinguishing skills from related Claude capabilities

We can now summarize how skills relate to **projects**, **connectors**, and **custom instructions**.

Skills activate dynamically when they are relevant, whereas projects are always loaded at the beginning of a chat started within that specific project. Projects therefore provide static background knowledge, while skills provide specialized procedures that work everywhere across Claude.

Skills contain procedural knowledge, which is how to do a task. **Connectors** provide access to external services and data, often through **Model Context Protocol (MCP)**. A connector gives Claude access to an external tool; a skill teaches Claude how to use that tool effectively as part of a workflow. We will examine connectors and MCP in a later chapter.

Custom instructions apply broadly to all your conversations, while skills are task-specific and load only when the current request is relevant. This makes *skills* more appropriate for specialized workflows that should not influence every conversation.

You do not need to call a skill by name. Instead, describe the task you want to accomplish. Suppose your account contains a skill for creating LinkedIn posts. A request such as `Help me create a LinkedIn post` can signal that the stored process is relevant, allowing Claude to activate it without requiring you to remember its exact name. Later chapters explain how this activation behavior can be refined and tested.

Understanding the four types of skills

There are four fundamental types of skills in the Claude ecosystem:

1. **Anthropic-generated skills**: These are created by Anthropic to demonstrate what Claude can do. You can find them in the **Customize** section, under **Skills**, then **Browse skills**. They are pre-created, labeled with Anthropic as the author, and can be installed with a single click. Examples include a **Slack GIF Creator** and **Skill Creator**, along with skills for working with tools such as Excel, Word, PowerPoint, and PDF.
2. **Custom skills**: These are the main focus of this book. You create custom skills for your own processes, giving Claude the knowledge to perform a specific task according to your workflow. Because they are built around the way you actually work, they are the best way to save time and increase productivity.
3. **Organization-provisioned skills**: These are relevant if you are part of an organization. Your admins can make certain skills available to everyone, for example, a branding skill. These appear automatically as organizational skills in your environment, and require no action from you to access.
4. **Partner skills**: These are developed by Anthropic partners and are generally designed to work with a partner's connector. For example, a CRM provider such as HubSpot, or a collaboration platform such as Slack, may provide skills that work with access to that service.

Finding existing skills

You can find many skills online. If you search for skills for a product manager or a growth marketer, you will find a large number that other people have created, which is possible because a *skill* is fundamentally a text file describing how a process is performed. The following are some popular skill marketplaces:

- **Smithery**: more than 120,000 skills, with verified quality indicators

- **SkillsMP**: more than 175,000 skills from the open `SKILL.md` ecosystem
- **SkillHub**: real-time trending skills, updated every six hours

At least at the beginning, it is better not to depend heavily on these skills. A skill is useful when it helps with an actual task and is built around the process you use to complete it. Existing skills can provide inspiration, and inspecting them can show how other people have organized their instructions, but the best practice is generally to create your own. The most valuable capability is not collecting a large number of skills from the internet; it is ***understanding how to create and use skills that reflect the way you already work***.

Summary

In this chapter, we placed skills within the four layers of the Claude ecosystem: interfaces, workspaces, native capabilities, and extensions. We then defined a *skill* as a reusable set of instructions that teaches Claude how to perform a specific task according to your processes, examples, formatting requirements, and quality standards.

We examined the structure of a skill, including the required `SKILL.md` file and the optional references, assets, and scripts that support more complex workflows. We also distinguished a standalone `.md` file from a packaged `.zip` or `.skill` archive containing `SKILL.md` and its supporting files.

We then compared skills with Projects, establishing that Projects provide the context for a body of work, while skills define the reusable process for completing a task. Finally, we explored how skills operate across Chat and Cowork, how they differ from connectors and custom instructions, and the four types of skills: Anthropic-generated, custom, organization-provisioned, and partner skills.

With this foundation in place, the next chapter introduces five methods for creating a skill, beginning with Skill Creator and the recommended approach of converting a successful task into a reusable workflow.

2

Five Methods for Creating Claude Skills

There are five fundamental ways to create a **Claude Skill**, and every one of them is valid. The method you reach for depends on what already exists when you begin. Sometimes you have only an *idea for a workflow*. In other cases you have already completed the task successfully, built the same workflow in another AI platform, documented a complex process in advance, or found a skill that someone else has already built.

Although all five methods are useful, one of them stands above the rest for day-to-day work: completing a task with Claude and then turning the successful result into a skill afterward. This method is time-efficient because it solves the task in front of you while also producing a process you can reuse later. We will still work through all five methods, so that you can pick the one that fits each situation, but Method 2 is the one to reach for most often.

In this chapter, we will cover the following topics:

- Choosing a skill creation method
- Using Skill Creator
- Turning a successful task into a skill
- Migrating an existing AI workflow
- Planning and designing a complex skill
- Importing and adapting an existing skill

Technical requirements

To follow the examples in this chapter, you will need the following:

- A Claude account with access to the **Customize** and **Skills** sections
- Access to **Claude Chat** or **Claude Cowork**
- Access to Claude Cowork and the **Claude in Chrome** extension for the browser-based migration demonstration. Cowork controls the browser through Claude in Chrome, so both are required

Some examples also use connected services, including **Gmail** and **Fathom**, a call-recording tool. These services support the demonstrated workflows, but the same creation methods apply to tasks that do not depend on external connections.

Choosing a skill creation method

The five methods for creating a skill are:

1. Use Claude's **Skill Creator**.
2. Complete a task with Claude, then turn it into a skill.
3. Migrate a **Custom GPT** or **Gemini Gem**.
4. Plan and design the skill in a `file`.
5. Import and adapt a skill someone else has built.

The first method begins with a description of the skill you want Claude to create. The second begins with the task itself and converts a successful result into a reusable process. The third moves an existing workflow from another AI platform into Claude. The fourth documents a complex process before the skill is built. The fifth starts from an existing skill and adapts it to a new environment.

Methods 1 and 2 are the ones most likely to be used in day-to-day work. Method 2 is the method I recommend most strongly, whether you are just getting started or are already much further along in working with Claude. Before we reach it, however, we will begin with the built-in process that Anthropic provides for creating skills.

Method 1: Using Skill Creator

Anthropic has created a process that captures its best practices for building skills, and that process is itself provided as a skill called Skill Creator. The idea can sound counterintuitive at first, because you use one skill to create another, but in practice it is straightforward.

Skill Creator is already available in every Claude account, whether you use Claude on your computer or in the browser, so there is nothing separate to build before you use it. Whenever Claude understands that the current task is to create a skill, it loads Skill Creator and uses its instructions to generate the new skill according to Anthropic's structure. You begin by describing what the skill should do, and the method works both for a relatively simple workflow, such as removing common AI patterns from text, and for a more practical workflow involving meetings, email, and scheduled execution.

Option A: Creating a skill from reference material

Suppose the goal is to create a skill that helps your text avoid sounding like AI. Rather than trying to define every unwanted expression by hand, you can point Claude at a reliable source containing the information you want the skill to use. Use the following prompt:

```
Help me create skills to avoid sounding like AI by using the knowledge inside this
article: https://isgpt.org/blog/ai-vocabulary-top-50
```

The referenced article lists phrases that frequently appear in AI-generated text. The source gives Skill Creator a useful body of information from which to build its instructions. Claude receives both the task the skill should perform and the source from which the rules should be derived, then uses that reference together with Skill Creator to generate the skill. *Figure 2.1* shows the prompt being entered in Claude Cowork.

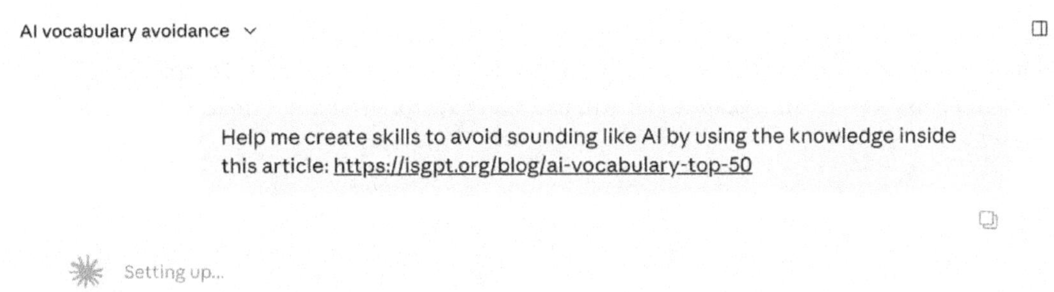

Figure 2.1: Entering the AI-vocabulary skill prompt in Claude Cowork

Skill Creator may ask you a few questions before building the skill. For example, it may ask what the skill should do when it detects a flagged phrase: only flag it, or flag and rewrite it. These clarification questions help define the intended behavior before Claude generates the instructions.

The same method applies to other tasks because the reference material does not have to be an *article about writing*. It can be any reliable source containing the knowledge the skill needs to perform its task.

Option B: Creating a connected skill from a prompt

The same method also works for a *workflow* that relies on external information. Instead of a skill that only processes text, you can describe a process that spans your calendar, external attendees, email history, and daily scheduling. Use the following prompt:

```
Use the skill-creator skill to create a skill to check the meetings that I have
today, understand the meetings that have an external person in the invite (my
domains are @notlinear.ai and @nforce.ai), and do a quick search over in my Gmail
for previous email exchanges I had with each person, and create a quick bullet
point list of points we discussed in chat.
```

This prompt defines several parts of the workflow at once. Claude has to check the meetings scheduled for the day, identify which invitations include people outside the specified domains (`@notlinear.ai` and `@nforce.ai`), search Gmail for earlier exchanges with those people, and return a short bullet-point list of what was discussed. You can then extend the workflow with a scheduling instruction so that it runs each morning:

```
Schedule the skill to run at 9AM every day.
```

This example is more advanced because it uses external information and several steps, but the basic creation process remains the same. You describe the task and make it clear that Claude should use Skill Creator. Claude then loads Skill Creator and may ask clarification questions before generating the new skill. In Cowork, the loaded skill is visible in the **Context** panel, as shown in *Figure 2.2*. In Chat, Claude can still use Skill Creator even if it is not displayed in the same way.

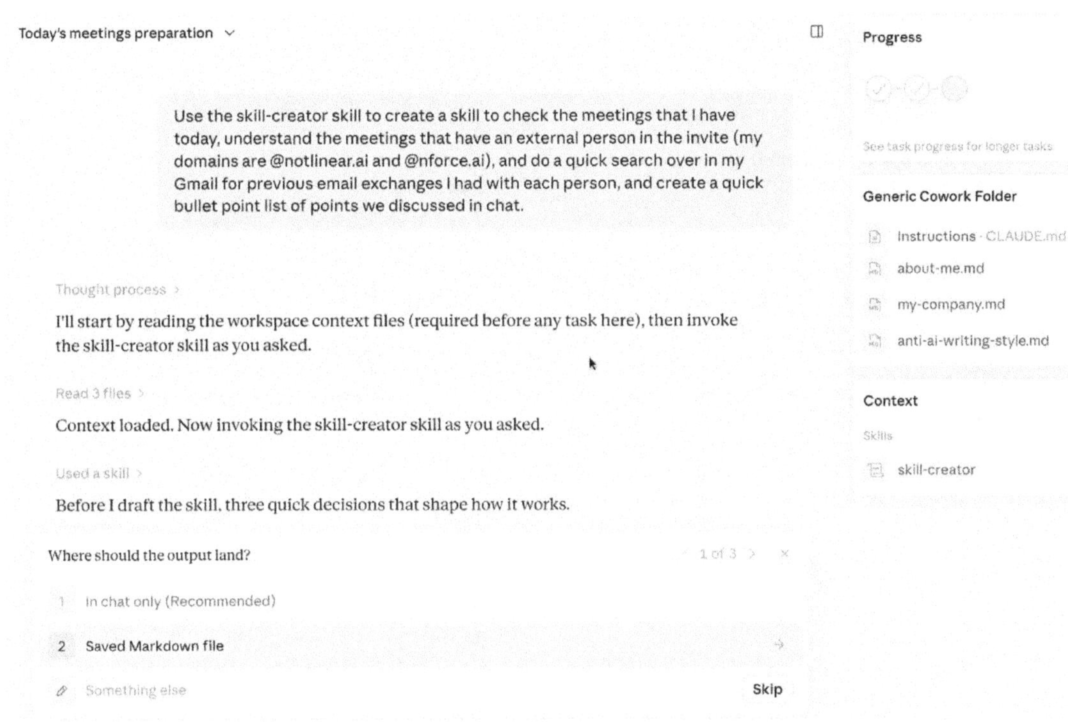

Figure 2.2: Skill Creator loaded in Cowork and asking where the generated skill should be saved

Reviewing and saving the generated skill

A skill that has been generated inside a conversation is not automatically available across your account. It must be saved. Claude may complete the full creation process and present a working `SKILL.md` file, but the skill will not appear in your **Skills** section until you complete the save action. *Figure 2.3* shows the generated `SKILL.md` file and the controls available for saving it.

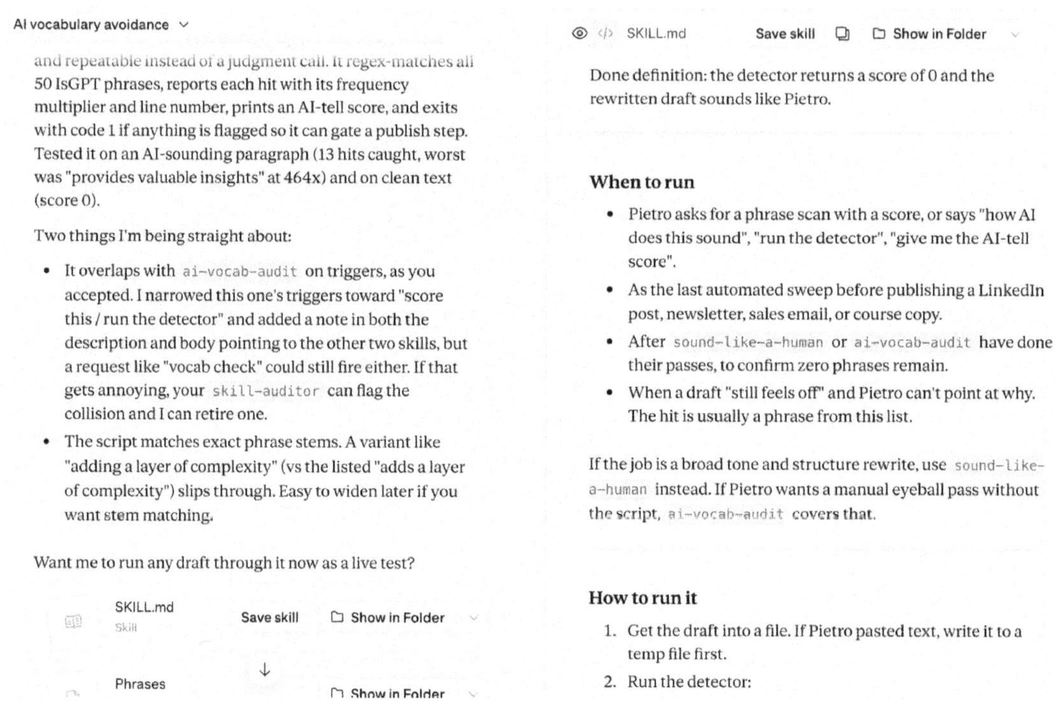

Figure 2.3: The generated SKILL.md file, with options to select Save skill or Show in Folder

When the save option is available, add the skill to your account by selecting **Save skill**. Once saved, it appears in **Customize** and can be used in other conversations. Occasionally Claude finishes generating a skill but offers only an option to download it. If the save button does not appear, give an additional instruction:

```
Give me this skill to save.
```

Claude can then return the skill in a form that provides the save option. The rule is simple: every skill creation process must end with saving the skill. If the skill is generated but not saved, it will not be available across your account, and the work done inside the conversation is effectively lost when you need the skill elsewhere.

Method 2: Turning a successful task into a skill

The second method is, in my opinion, the best possible way to create skills, and it is the one I strongly recommend for day-to-day work, both when you are getting started and after you have gained more experience.

Instead of beginning with a request such as `Help me create a skill`, you begin by performing the actual task with Claude. You complete it exactly as you would normally use AI: you provide the material, explain what you need, review the response, correct it, and continue until the result is satisfactory. Only after the task has been completed successfully do you turn it into a skill.

This sequence matters because the first run exposes the real process. It reveals the information Claude needs, the decisions that have to be made, the corrections that come up, and the shape of an output you are willing to accept. The skill is therefore built from a working example rather than from an imagined specification.

Completing the task before creating the skill

Suppose the task is to generate an invoice or create a presentation. You first give Claude all the material it needs. For a presentation, this may include the source information, the context, and the requirements for the output.

A back-and-forth follows. You might tell Claude that a particular direction is not right, add a source, ask for a different structure, or request a more concise result. None of this begins as a skill creation process; it is simply the ordinary work of completing a task with Claude, and it continues until the output is successful. The basic pattern is:

1. Perform the task with Claude.
2. Provide the required materials, context, and feedback.
3. Continue until the output is satisfactory.
4. Ask Claude to create a skill from the completed process.
5. Review and save the skill.

The first time you perform the task, the immediate goal is to finish the work. The reusable process is created only after that goal has been reached.

Building a follow-up email with Claude

To see the method in practice, consider a sales workflow that begins right after a call with an external person. The first task is to understand what happened during the call. Claude has access to the call transcript through Fathom, a call-recording tool similar to other meeting-recording services, and it also has access to Gmail. The process begins with a request to review the call:

```
Give me a rundown of the key topics I talked about with this person.
```

Claude uses the Fathom recording to identify the topics discussed and the resulting action items. The next request is to draft a follow-up email. At this stage you explain the structure you want, and the email should contain the sections and information that matter after the call. In the demonstration, the follow-up email to Lucy is organized into three sections:

- What we discussed
- As promised
- Next steps

Claude produces a first version, but the interaction does not stop there. As with any ordinary Claude task, you review and correct the output; the email may need a different format, a shorter length, or additional detail. During the process, Claude notices that a discount code was promised on the call but has not yet been provided. It asks for the missing code, and the code is added to the email. *Figure 2.4* shows the completed email after these revisions.

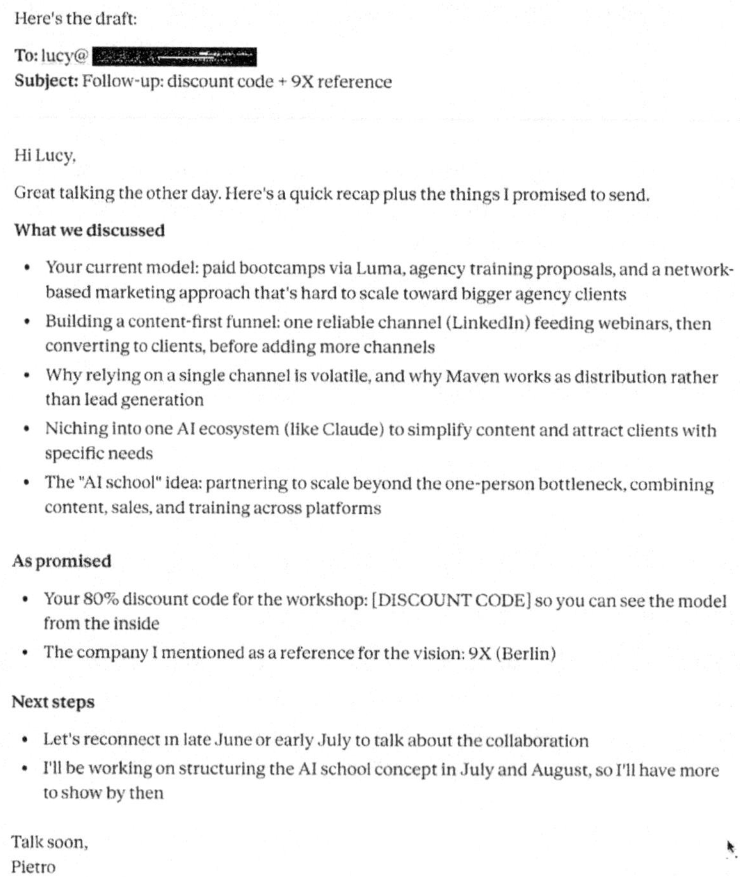

Here's the draft:

To: lucy@

Subject: Follow-up: discount code + 9X reference

Hi Lucy,

Great talking the other day. Here's a quick recap plus the things I promised to send.

What we discussed

- Your current model: paid bootcamps via Luma, agency training proposals, and a network-based marketing approach that's hard to scale toward bigger agency clients
- Building a content-first funnel: one reliable channel (LinkedIn) feeding webinars, then converting to clients, before adding more channels
- Why relying on a single channel is volatile, and why Maven works as distribution rather than lead generation
- Niching into one AI ecosystem (like Claude) to simplify content and attract clients with specific needs
- The "AI school" idea: partnering to scale beyond the one-person bottleneck, combining content, sales, and training across platforms

As promised

- Your 80% discount code for the workshop: [DISCOUNT CODE] so you can see the model from the inside
- The company I mentioned as a reference for the vision: 9X (Berlin)

Next steps

- Let's reconnect in late June or early July to talk about the collaboration
- I'll be working on structuring the AI school concept in July and August, so I'll have more to show by then

Talk soon,
Pietro

Figure 2.4: The completed follow-up email, organized into What we discussed, As promised, and Next steps

The work continues until the email has the right structure, includes the required information, and is concise enough for its purpose. If the result is not yet right, the back-and-forth continues. You should not create the skill from output you have not accepted.

Converting the successful task into a skill

Once the final email is satisfactory, you can ask Claude to convert the process into a reusable skill:

```
Based on the content of this conversation, please generate a skill to follow up on
any sales conversation which I have.
```

Claude then calls Skill Creator and reads the full context of the conversation. This includes the original request, the Fathom call information, the structure requested for the email, the corrections made along the way, the additional discount-code requirement, and the final successful output. The skill is built from this complete history, so it inherits what made the task work: the voice, the format, the process, the materials, and the connected services.

This method therefore produces two results at once. The immediate follow-up email is already finished, so the work required for the day is done, and the process has been packaged into a skill you can use after the next sales call. The same approach applies to other work. Once a presentation has been completed successfully, its process can be turned into a skill for producing the same type of presentation later, and the same can be done for an invoice, a report, or any other repeated task. As with Method 1, the new skill must be saved before it becomes available for later use.

Reusing the skill in another conversation

Once the follow-up skill has been saved, it can be called from anywhere in your Claude account. It does not need to be used in the conversation where it was created. For example, an earlier conversation may have been about creating the AI-vocabulary skill from Method 1. Even in that unrelated conversation, the saved follow-up skill can be invoked:

```
Use the follow-up skill to generate follow-up for my latest Fathom call.
```

Claude recognizes the saved skill, loads the follow-up email instructions, checks your most recent meeting, and applies the process captured during the earlier successful task, regardless of the current conversation topic.

Any skill you save through this method appears in your **Customize** section. Skills you create yourself are listed under **Personal skills**. If you are part of a team or organization account, you may also see **Built-in skills**, which are provided as part of Claude, and **Organization skills**, which an administrator has made available to members of the organization. When you save a skill, it is stored in your Anthropic account in the cloud, so it remains available whether you work in Claude Chat or Claude Cowork, or when you sign in from another computer or through the browser.

A skill is never truly finished; skills improve through iteration. If a later output is not satisfactory, you can edit the skill through conversation, for example, by telling Claude that you do not like the current output and asking it to move the skill in a different direction. Claude generates an updated version, which you then save over the earlier one. Every edit has to reach the save stage, or the change stays inside the current conversation and is lost.

Why this method works

This method is the strongest recommendation because it is both practical and time-efficient. The task you need to complete today is finished first, and if that task recurs, the successful process is then available for the next time. You are not spending effort on a skill before you know whether the process works.

Beginning with the finished task also gives a much better sense of how the process actually performs. Completing the work first reveals which information is missing, the kind of input the task requires, and which parts of the output need correction. Designing a skill from an imagined specification, before running the task even once, gives you none of that feedback.

Sharing a skill across accounts

A saved skill can be downloaded and shared with another person, but the same `Skill` file does not always produce exactly the same output in another account. Claude retains information about each account: the general settings may hold instructions describing who you are and how Claude should behave, and **Memory** holds information Claude has retained over time. This account-level context contributes to the result alongside the instructions inside the skill.

If you create a `meeting-notes` skill and share it with a colleague, their output may be similar without being identical, because the receiving account may hold instructions or memory that differ from yours, and any conflict with the skill can cause the output to deviate. Two steps reduce this problem:

- Tell Claude clearly that you are building the skill for your full team and intend to share it, so that it excludes personal information about you from the *skill* body.
- Make sure the recipient runs the skill with the same model version you used when creating it, for example, **Haiku 4.5** versus **Opus 4.8**, since different models can produce significantly different results.

Making the model match is the simplest and most important fix, and it is worth confirming before comparing outputs across accounts.

Method 3: Migrating an existing AI workflow

The third method is useful when you have already built work in **ChatGPT**, **Gemini**, or another AI platform. Instead of recreating the workflow by hand, Claude can inspect the existing assistant, extract its process, and convert it into a skill.

A direct migration can begin by pasting the existing material:

```
Use the skill creator to help me turn a custom GPT into a skill. I will now paste
the system prompt and files.
```

For a larger batch of **Custom GPTs**, use the following prompt:

```
Browse to ChatGPT, explore all of my custom GPTs and ask me which I want to
convert into a skill, then convert the selected ones using the skills creator
skill.
```

A similar prompt can be used for **Projects**:

```
Browse to ChatGPT, explore all of my custom projects and ask me which I want to
convert into a skill, then convert the selected ones using the skills creator
skill.
```

Claude begins by reading the available workspace context, preparing the task, and opening ChatGPT through Claude in Chrome, as shown in *Figure 2.5*.

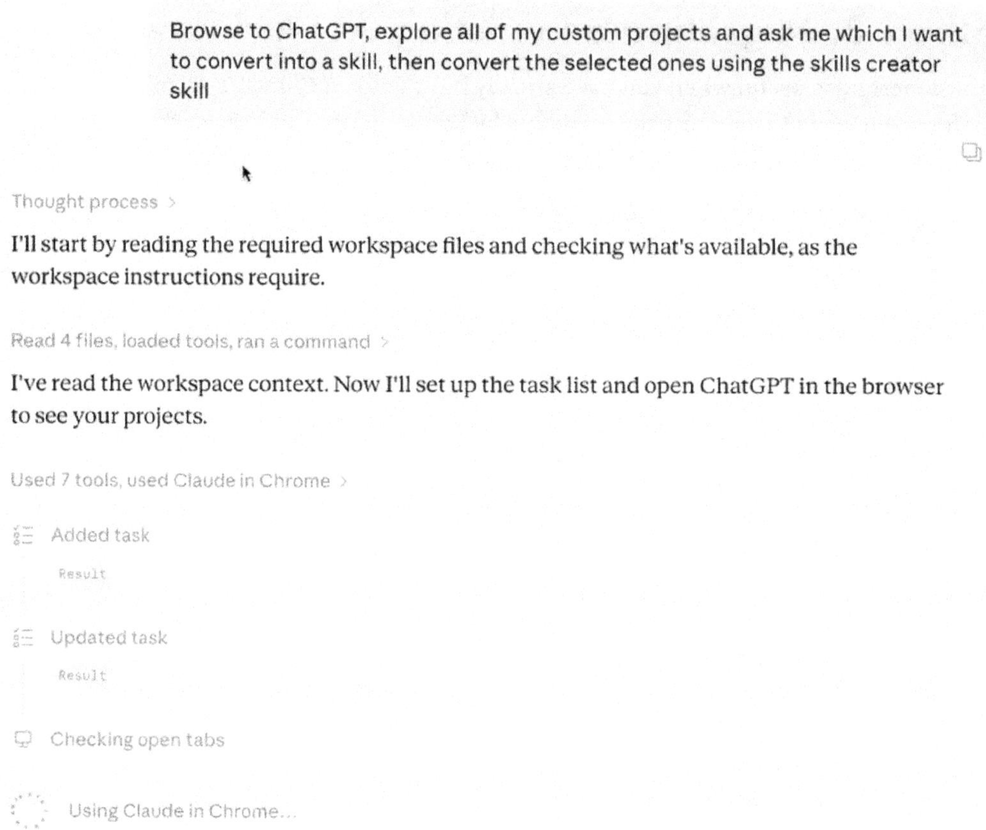

Figure 2.5: Cowork preparing the migration task and opening ChatGPT through Claude in Chrome

Once the external platform opens, Cowork can interact with the active browser tab on your behalf. As shown in *Figure 2.6*, the control banner and orange outline indicate that Claude is controlling the ChatGPT **Projects** page.

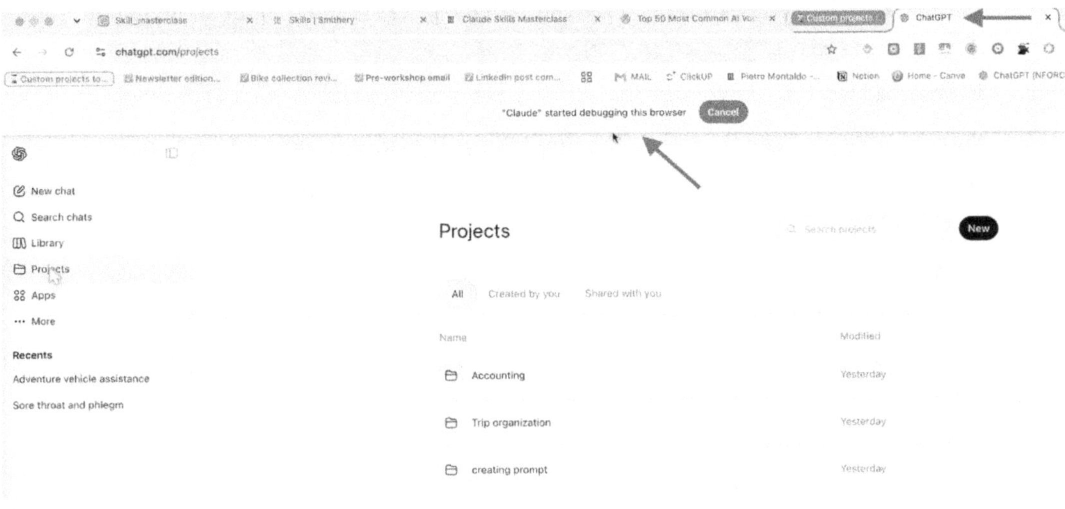

Figure 2.6: Cowork controlling the ChatGPT Projects page during the migration workflow

Claude can then inspect the selected Project's instructions and files and use Skill Creator to build the equivalent Claude skill. This approach is essentially a one-off workaround for moving existing assets into Claude, and it is generally needed only when you are transitioning from another platform. For ongoing work, Methods 1 and 2 remain more relevant, and of those two, Method 2 is still the most effective and time-efficient recommendation.

Method 4: Planning and designing a complex skill

In a small number of cases it makes sense to design a skill in a document before asking Claude to create it. This is an exception rather than the default, and it is appropriate for a particularly complex skill, a sophisticated process, or a skill that will be shared across hundreds of people, where you want tight control over what goes into each part of the skill.

The design can be written on paper, in a **Google Doc**, or in another file. Fundamentally, the document provides Claude with the following nine sets of information, grouped under identity (name, trigger, goal), context (connectors, reference files), process (step-by-step process, human-in-the-loop, output), and learning (progressive updates):

1. **Name**: what you call the skill. Use a clear, recognizable, lowercase-hyphenated format.
2. **Trigger**: the exact phrases or intent that should activate the skill, so Claude knows when to load it.
3. **Goal**: one sentence describing what the skill produces.

4. **Connectors**: the MCPs, APIs, or tools the skill uses. Name the specific table or endpoint if it matters.
5. **Reference files**: the knowledge the skill reads when it runs, listed by `filename`.
6. **Step-by-step process**: the execution flow; this is the most important section.
7. **Human-in-the-loop**: where the skill should pause for your input, using a Q&A box such as a **checkbox**, **single-select**, or **open field**.
8. **Output**: what the final output is and where it lives.
9. **Progressive updates** (optional): the rule that makes the skill `self-learning`.

The first three elements define the skill's identity: the **name** gives it a recognizable label, the **trigger** tells Claude when to load it, and the **goal** states what it is meant to achieve.

The context section identifies the **connectors** that provide access to external systems and the **reference files** that supply supporting knowledge, such as examples of successful emails, previous presentations, or brand materials.

The **step-by-step process** is the key part of the design, because it describes what Claude should do and in what order. When you design the process, you can also define **human-in-the-loop** steps, which simply means involving yourself in the workflow. For instance, you can instruct Claude to pause after the first draft:

```
Once you have finished the first draft, check with me whether I like the
direction. Otherwise, let us edit it together.
```

The same principle applies when you delegate to an intern who checks with you before sending something to a partner. At the beginning, I recommend staying as involved as possible, because frequent checkpoints make it easier to confirm the skill is heading in the right direction and to steer it when the output begins to drift. The trade-off is that you must remain available to review and approve the work, but this early involvement builds your confidence in the process, and you can reduce it later as the skill becomes more dependable.

The **output section** defines the final result. It may specify whether the skill produces an Excel file, a PowerPoint presentation, or another artifact, along with formatting details such as fonts. For an ambitious or complex task, you write all of these decisions down before the skill is built. Once the document contains the complete design, you hand it to Claude with an instruction such as:

```
Using this information, help me design a skill that adheres exactly to all of the
information I have included.
```

Claude then uses Skill Creator to turn the documented process into a skill. This method takes more time than completing a task and converting it afterward, so it is reserved for exceptional cases. It is also useful for understanding what Skill Creator does internally, because whenever Claude creates a skill, it is effectively filling in these same nine sections from the information available in the conversation.

Method 5: Importing and adapting an existing skill

The fifth method begins with a skill someone else has already built. It may come from a teammate, the *downloadable sample skill bundle provided with this book*, **Anthropic's Skills directory**, or an external repository such as **Smithery**. This method is useful when an existing skill already resembles the workflow you need and can serve as a starting point for your own version.

> NOTE
>
> To access the downloadable sample skill bundle, see the *Download the sample skill bundle* section in the Preface.

When you receive or download a `skill` file, open **Customize**, select **Skills**, click the plus (+) button, choose **Create skill**, and then select **Upload a skill**, as shown in *Figure 2.7*. Make sure the file uses one of the supported formats introduced in *Chapter 1*. After Claude imports the file, the skill appears under **Personal skills**.

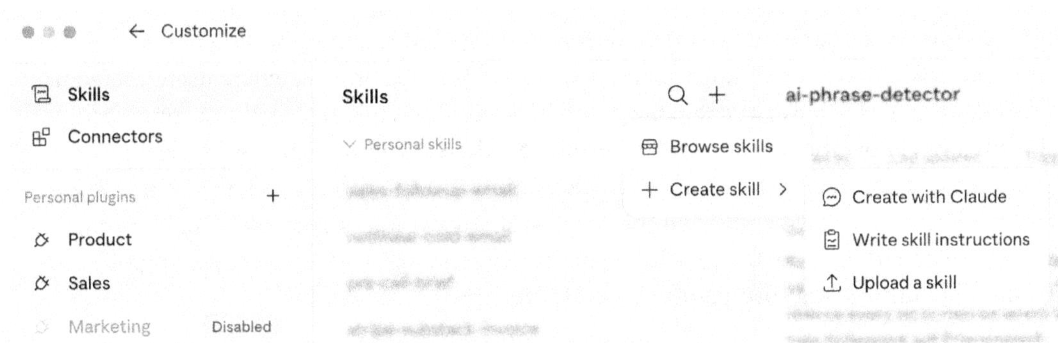

Figure 2.7: The Skills menu showing Browse skills and the Create skill | Upload a skill path

Importing the file is only the first stage. An external skill should not be expected to create value the moment it is installed because it was built in someone else's environment and may reflect a different process, organization, or set of assumptions. Every imported skill therefore needs two phases: **understanding** and **adaptation**.

The *understanding phase* establishes what the skill does and how its process works so that you can edit it collaboratively later. This matters most when a skill comes from outside your organization. A skill shared within your own team may already reflect your environment and need little adjustment, while one downloaded from a public repository is more likely to require substantial changes.

Once you understand the structure, Claude can customize the skill for your business or workflow, regardless of where it came from. To demonstrate this process, open **Browse skills** and install Anthropic's Brand Guidelines skill as an example. Then open a new task and use the following prompt:

```
Help me understand and customize the Brand Guidelines skill from Anthropic to my
business. I just downloaded it.
```

The prompt tells Claude that you have obtained the skill and want help understanding and adapting it. Claude reviews the skill, explains how its process works, identifies the information it needs, and begins customizing it for your business. If you are working in Cowork and have already provided context about your company, yourself, and your writing style, Claude can use that information directly and may not need to ask for additional details.

When the *adaptation is complete*, save the updated skill so that the revised version overrides the imported one and your changes are available in later conversations.

Summary

In this chapter, we examined five methods for creating Claude Skills. Method 1 uses Anthropic's Skill Creator to build a skill from a direct description and, where useful, reference material, and we saw how the same method scales from a simple text skill to a connected, scheduled workflow that checks daily meetings. Method 2 begins with a real task: we completed a follow-up email workflow using Fathom and Gmail, refined it until the output was satisfactory, and then converted the successful process into a reusable skill. This remains the recommended method, because it finishes the immediate work while capturing the decisions, materials, and corrections needed for future runs.

We then looked at migrating Custom GPTs, Gemini Gems, and Projects into Claude Skills as a one-off step when moving from another platform. For complex or widely distributed workflows, we examined a design method built on nine elements grouped under identity, context, process, and learning. Finally, we imported Anthropic's Brand Guidelines skill and adapted it to a new business context. Across every method, one rule holds: a skill must be saved before it appears in the **Customize** section and becomes available across the account. Output can also be influenced by the model version and the account-specific context that each

Claude account brings to the skill. With these creation methods in place, we are ready to look next at the design decisions that keep skills focused and efficient. The next chapter examines skill length, human-in-the-loop checkpoints, examples, reference files, triggers, and the point at which one large skill should be divided into several smaller workflows.

3

Designing Focused and Efficient Skills

Creating a skill is only the starting point. A skill becomes genuinely useful through repeated use, correction, and refinement, and the first version rarely needs to perform the whole workflow perfectly. Expecting that level of completeness from the outset is one of the most common reasons a skill is built and then never used.

The most effective skills share three characteristics. They stay focused on a single job, they keep their core instructions short, and they keep us involved at the points where our judgment or our material still matters. As the workflow becomes more dependable, the skill can absorb more of the repetitive work. The aim is not to remove ourselves from the process straight away, but to become faster and more effective by directing it. In this sense, we remain the *orchestrator* rather than the operator.

This chapter sets out the design principles that keep a skill focused and efficient: how to size it, when to split it, how to keep its `instruction file` lean, how to run and trigger it, and how to choose which work is worth turning into a skill in the first place.

In this chapter, we will cover the following topics:

- Designing a focused skill
- Controlling skill length and context
- Running and triggering skills
- Choosing what to turn into a skill
- Teaching Claude work that is already understood

Technical requirements

No additional setup is required beyond the **Claude account** and the **Skills** access used in the previous chapters. The scheduling example later in the chapter relies on **Claude Cowork**, because recurring **Scheduled Tasks** are available there but not in Claude Chat. Everything else can be followed in either interface.

Designing a focused skill

The first principle to keep in mind is that a skill should do only one job. A skill should not be handed several different responsibilities simply because those responsibilities belong to the same broader process. When a single skill tries to cover three or four tasks, pieces of the process tend to be lost as it runs. Claude receives more instructions, more context, and more possible directions at once, and that makes it harder to stay focused on the intended result. Keeping the skill narrow gives Claude a clearer process to follow and makes the expected output more likely.

Keeping a skill focused does not mean that its first version must be complete. Begin with a simple working skill, use it whenever the task recurs, and expect to refine it over five to ten or more iterations. Early versions should also keep us involved wherever our information, judgment, or approval is still required.

Starting with a simple version

A skill should begin simply. Demanding a perfect skill from the first attempt creates a barrier to using it at all, whereas a basic working version can immediately take part of the effort out of a repeated task. The first version can start with plain instructions written in `Markdown`, with more complex scripts and supporting components added later as the workflow matures.

The pattern is straightforward. We complete the task with Claude, turn the successful result into a skill, and then use that skill the next time the task comes around. The second use often reveals a missing rule or an output that still needs too much correction, and that feedback becomes the basis for the next version. At the beginning, the skill simply makes the task faster and removes some of the work. Over time, as the instructions, references, and examples improve, it can take on more of that work. ***The important point is not to expect the first version to be one hundred percent complete.*** A skill that goes unused because it is not yet perfect can never learn from real work.

Remaining involved through human-in-the-loop checkpoints

Especially in the early versions, a skill should be designed to work alongside us. Whether the workflow drafts an email sequence, develops a product, or produces a document, there will be moments when a specific input, a particular sentence, a file, or a link is essential to getting the work right. Those moments should be visible in the process so that the skill can pause and ask for what it needs, rather than guessing or producing an incomplete result. Q&A boxes, checkboxes, and open fields can all be used to collect the required input before execution continues.

This is the purpose of *human-in-the-loop* checkpoints. We stay involved where our judgment, information, or approval matters, while the skill handles the repeatable work around those checkpoints. The same principle applies when work is delegated to a person: an intern might prepare a first draft but ask for approval before sending it to a partner. A skill can follow the same structure, pausing after the draft and waiting for confirmation before it proceeds. The instruction inside the skill might read:

```
Once you have finished the first draft, check with me whether I like the
direction. Otherwise, let us edit it together.
```

Early involvement makes it easier to confirm that the workflow is heading in the right direction and to correct it before the final output is produced. As confidence in the skill grows, some checkpoints can be removed and the workflow becomes more automated. That reduction should follow repeated successful use, not come before it.

Using examples to define success

Examples help Claude understand what a successful output actually looks like. Instructions can describe a format, a tone, or a process, but a previously approved result gives Claude a far more concrete picture of the target. In a simple skill, example inputs and outputs can start out inside `SKILL.md`. They are especially valuable when the task depends on voice, formatting, or branding, which are difficult to communicate through rules alone.

If the core file grows too long, those examples can later move into the `references/` folder and load only when the workflow needs them. Examples do not replace the process; they support it by showing how the instructions should appear in the finished result. As the skill produces successful outputs, selected results can be saved as approved examples for later runs.

Testing as the skill develops

Testing should happen after each meaningful change rather than after a large skill has already been assembled. If several layers of complexity are added before the first real test, it becomes difficult to tell which instruction sent the workflow in the wrong direction. Incremental testing keeps the link between a change and its outcome visible.

In practice, we add or revise part of the skill, use it on a real task, inspect the result, and decide whether the change improved the process. This practical feedback is what moves the skill toward dependable performance. The formal evaluation methods are covered in the next chapter; at this stage the principle is simply to avoid building an extensive workflow without checking it along the way.

Controlling skill length and context

Anthropic recommends that ***a skill should not exceed 500 lines***. Treat this as a red line rather than a target. Every line in a skill competes with the current conversation for space in the context window, so the more focused and concise the skill is, the better its output is likely to be.

Claude already understands common concepts and file types. A skill does not need to explain what a PDF is or restate general information that Claude already has. It should include only the context that is specific to the workflow and unavailable without the skill. The length is easy to check by asking Claude directly:

```
How long is my skill?
```

If the answer is more than 500 lines, there is a strong chance the skill is trying to do too much. At that point the process should be reviewed to find instructions, supporting information, or separate jobs that do not belong in the core skill.

Recognizing an overloaded skill

Length is one indicator, but the quality of the output is usually the clearest signal. When the result is not professional, does not match the intended direction, or is not something we would be comfortable sharing externally, the skill may be too extensive or may be attempting several jobs at once. Too much context causes Claude to lose focus, and once focus slips, quality declines.

This does not mean every disappointing output comes down to length, but it is a strong reason to check whether the skill still holds one clear responsibility. A skill may be too extensive when:

- It performs more than one job.
- Its output shifts substantially depending on the context.
- It contains too many "but only when" conditions.
- Quality falls as more instructions and exceptions are added.

When these signs appear, review the skill for two things: whether every instruction supports the same job and whether any part of the workflow can run independently. The second question determines whether the skill should remain intact or be divided into smaller skills.

Splitting a larger workflow

Consider a sales workflow built around a list of leads. The full process might include:

- Researching every lead
- Drafting an outreach message
- Sending that message through a third-party tool

These activities all contribute to one broader sales process, but they are not one job. Placed inside a single skill, they produce a long skill that has to research, write, and operate an external delivery tool all at once, and each stage brings its own instructions, information, and possible points of failure.

A more focused design separates the work into three **skills**:

- One skill for lead research
- One skill for drafting the outreach message
- One skill for sending the message

The three pieces can still run together as part of one broader process, but each skill stays responsible for a single focused job. The research output becomes an input for drafting, and the approved draft becomes an input for sending. The decision comes down to whether the steps always occur together. If they are inseparable and consistently form one task, they can stay in one skill. If they sometimes happen independently, they should be split and then connected as part of a larger process. When several skills need to be packaged or coordinated together, a plugin can provide that next layer, but plugins fall outside the scope of this chapter.

Keeping SKILL.md focused on core logic

A skill can grow long even when it performs only one job. This happens when every supporting rule, guideline, and example is placed inside `SKILL.md`. The file may begin with the *core instructions* but gradually expand to include brand guidelines, tone-of-voice requirements, MCP guidance, formatting rules, and examples. Because all of this material sits inside the core file, it loads whenever the skill runs, making the skill longer and consuming context even when some of the information is not needed.

A better structure keeps the execution logic in `SKILL.md` and moves supporting material into a separate `references/` folder. This folder sits beside `SKILL.md` within the main `Skill` folder. It is not contained inside the `SKILL.md` file. *Figure 3.1* shows the change from a single overloaded file to a shorter core file supported by separate references.

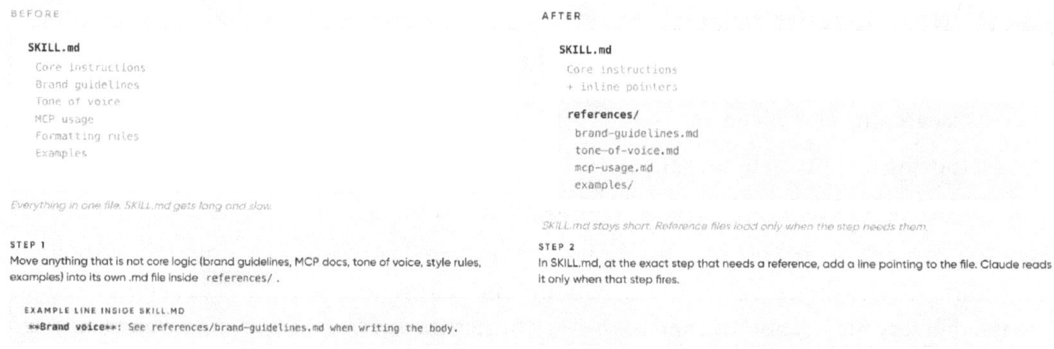

Figure 3.1: Moving supporting material out of SKILL.md and loading it only when needed

There are three changes to notice in the figure. First, `SKILL.md` retains the core instructions that control the workflow. Second, supporting information such as brand guidelines, tone rules, MCP guidance, and examples move into separate files inside `references/`. Third, the core instructions retain inline pointers that tell Claude which reference to read and when to read it.

The example at the bottom of the figure shows how such a pointer works. The brand guidance is no longer written directly into the core file. Instead, the relevant step directs Claude to `references/brand-guidelines.md` when it begins writing the body. The reference is therefore available when needed without occupying the core skill context throughout the entire workflow.

This approach does not remove useful context. It places each piece of information where it becomes relevant. `SKILL.md` remains focused on the process, while the reference files preserve the supporting knowledge required to complete the task.

Running and triggering skills

A reusable process can be started manually or, in Cowork, scheduled to run automatically. The right mechanism depends on the interface and how the work needs to begin.

Scheduling a skill in Cowork

Cowork provides Scheduled Tasks, which allow a process to run automatically at a recurring time. A skill defines what Claude should do, while the Scheduled Task determines when that process should begin. A recurring HubSpot or Asana check, for example, can first be captured in a skill and then scheduled to run hourly, daily, on weekdays, or weekly.

A scheduling request might take the form:

```
Run the HubSpot skill every Monday at 9 a.m.
```

To create a scheduled task:

1. **Open Scheduled** from the Cowork sidebar.
2. Select **New task**, then choose whether to create the task with Claude or set it up manually.

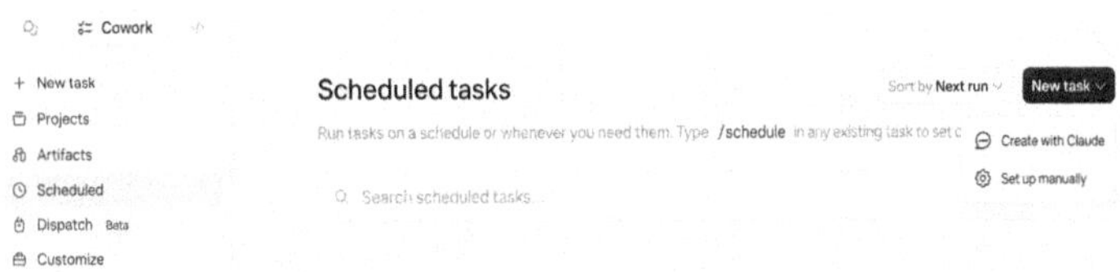

Figure 3.2: Opening the setup options for a scheduled task

The **Scheduled area** holds the tasks that run automatically or can be started when needed. Selecting **New task** provides the option to create the schedule with Claude or configure its details manually.

1. **Give the task a clear name**, add a short description, and enter the instruction that tells Claude which process to run.
2. Open the **Frequency** menu and choose how often the task should run. Complete any remaining required information, and then select **Save**.

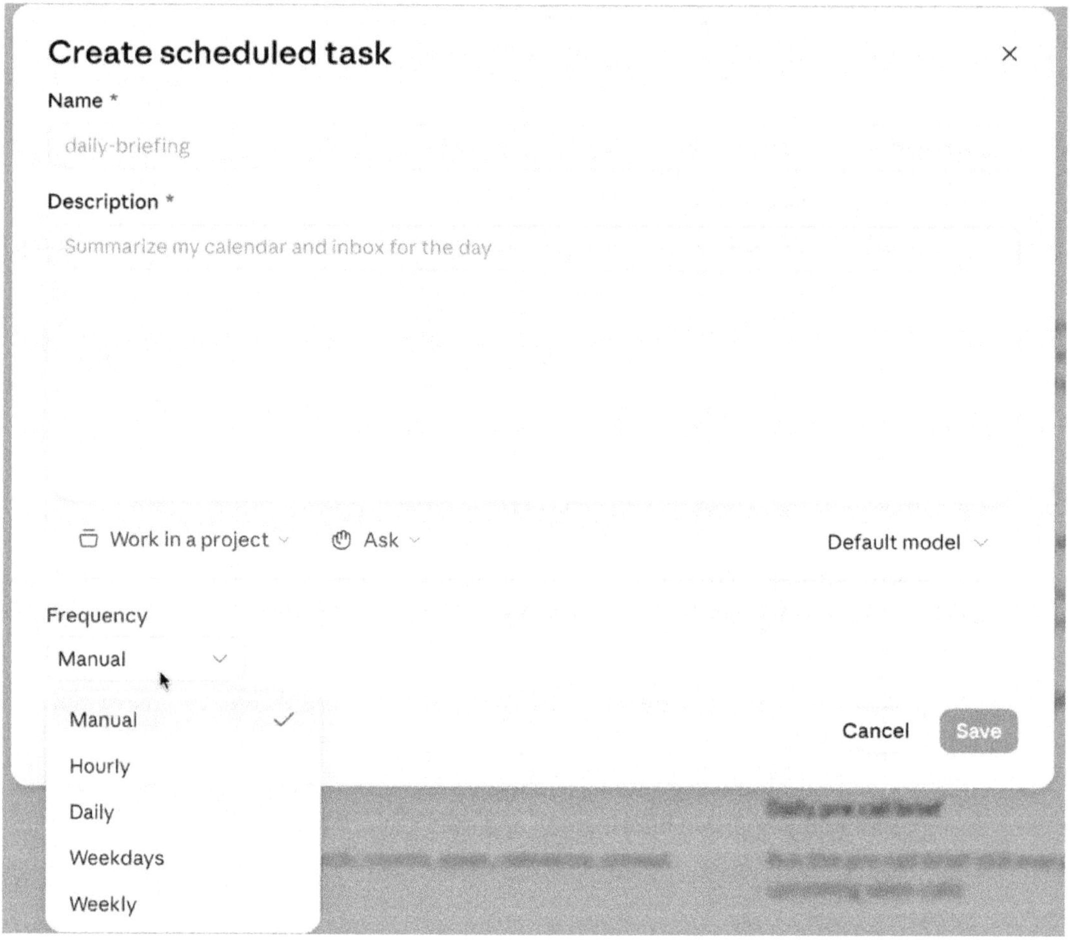

Figure 3.3: Adding the task details and choosing how often it should run

The task name identifies the scheduled workflow, while the description summarizes its purpose. Use the larger instruction field to specify the skill or process Claude should run. The **Frequency** menu determines whether the task runs manually, hourly, daily, on weekdays, or weekly. After completing the required details, select **Save** to create the task.

Cowork uses the schedule to start the process at the chosen time, while the skill continues to define what Claude should do once the task begins. **Scheduling** is specific to Cowork. Claude Chat can create and use skills, but it does not provide the same recurring Scheduled Tasks capability. This limitation applies only to automatic scheduling, not to creating, triggering, or using the skill normally.

Understanding the trigger

Every skill includes a **trigger** inside its initial description. The trigger tells Claude when the process should become active, and it can be thought of as an alarm that describes the task the skill performs and the kinds of requests that should wake it. For a sales follow-up skill, the description might tell Claude to use the skill when someone wants to follow up on a sales call, send a recap to a prospect, or draft a follow-up. Requests such as the following would then activate it:

- `Follow up with Lucy.`
- `Draft a follow-up.`
- `Send Lucy a recap.`

The request does not need to repeat the skill's name, because Claude matches the intent of the request against the description stored in the skill. In **Cowork**, a skill can be paired with a schedule; outside Cowork, we prompt it directly or discuss a task related to it. In both cases the **trigger** matters, because it tells Claude that the stored process applies to the current request. Clear descriptions are therefore important, since a vague description makes Claude's decision about when to load the skill less reliable. Trigger quality is tested more formally in the next chapter.

Scheduling and automatic triggering do not remove the need to direct the work. They shift our role from completing every repetitive step to managing the AI processes that carry out work with us or for us. Claude can help us move faster, do more, and produce higher-quality work, but we remain responsible for where the process goes and how the work is completed.

Choosing what to turn into a skill

There is no single skill that everyone should build first. The useful starting point depends on the work done each day and on where the largest share of repetitive effort currently sits. In my own work, one of the skills I use most is also one of the simplest: a skill that removes AI language patterns from text. Whenever I write an email or anything else, I do not want to fall back on those phrases, so the skill stays relevant across most of the work I do in Claude.

I also run almost all of my work through my Claude account. I can inspect a **HubSpot** pipeline, work with email, and read dashboards without repeatedly leaving the environment. For the organization I run, repetitive back-office processes such as contracting, invoicing, and meeting preparation are handled entirely through carefully designed skills. Those skills have become sophisticated precisely because they have been used and refined until they work well.

These examples reflect my own day-to-day work, and the right starting point in another role may be different. The useful question is: where do we spend most of our time on repetitive work? The next time one of those tasks appears, it can be completed with Claude, and once the result is accepted, the process can be turned into a skill using the method from the previous chapter. The step that follows is to commit to using that skill whenever the task recurs and to keep improving it until the workflow can handle most of the repetition.

External tools offer another starting point. If an organization works through **Asana**, HubSpot, or another connected system, the repeated activities performed inside that tool are strong candidates for skill-based workflows. The relationship between skills and **connectors** is examined in a later chapter.

Teaching Claude work that is already understood

A skill cannot be taught well when the underlying task is not yet understood. If I begin something entirely new, my approach is to start manually. Claude can help at different points, but I first need to see what works.

Consider writing for LinkedIn. It is usually easy to tell when a post has been generated by AI rather than written in the author's own style. If someone has not yet developed a personal approach to writing for LinkedIn, there is no established process or voice to place inside a skill. The first step is therefore to write manually and discover what works. Once several posts have performed well, they can be collected in a database. The more examples we provide, and the more context we give about what good output looks like, the better Claude can reproduce those characteristics.

At a fundamental level, *AI models* forecast the most likely word to follow the words that came before it, so they tend to return the most likely answer. If the objective is originality, a distinct personal voice, or a recognizable brand, Claude needs enough context about who we are and what we want to produce. Without that context, the output stays close to the most likely answer. It will not make us an outlier; it will place us in the middle, which is exactly what we do not want when building a personal brand or creating original content.

The path can feel counterintuitive. We first develop the work manually until we understand our own style and know what a successful output looks like; only then do we turn that process into a reusable skill. This is not limited to content. A process performed for ten years can often be taught to Claude in hours or minutes, depending on its complexity. When the process is not understood, Claude cannot supply the secret to succeeding, making money, or becoming better at the job; it can only return the most likely answer available from the request and the context.

NOTE

Preserving personal contribution

Claude is an instrument for moving faster, not a substitute for every part of our work. As a non-technical professional, a realistic goal is to increase productivity by two or three times by handing repetitive tasks that do not require creativity, personality, or individual judgment to skills. This creates more time for the activities where personal input genuinely matters.

In my case, that means developing new material, running live sessions, teaching, and writing posts that draw on more of my own input. Repetitive operational work can move to skills once the process has been understood and designed correctly. Skills do not create a perfect newsletter, presentation, or LinkedIn post by replacing the person responsible for it. They make us much faster at work we already understand and care about.

Summary

In this chapter, we examined the *design principles* that keep skills focused and efficient. A skill should perform one job, begin as a simple working version, and improve through repeated use rather than being expected to reach perfect performance immediately.

We saw why early workflows should keep us involved. Human-in-the-loop checkpoints, approved examples, and incremental testing let us direct the process while the skill takes over the repetitive parts, and some of that involvement can be reduced as the workflow becomes dependable.

We used Anthropic's 500-line recommendation as a practical boundary and examined how overloaded skills lose focus when they hold several jobs or too much context. Larger workflows can be divided into focused skills, while supporting guidance can move out of `SKILL.md` and into reference files that load only when required.

Finally, we explored recurring schedules, skill triggers, and the selection of useful tasks for automation. The strongest starting point is repeated work that is already understood, while new or creative work should first be developed manually so that the process, examples, and personal judgment needed for success can be captured accurately.

The next chapter introduces the **quality loop** used to decide whether a skill is ready for dependable use. We will work with **evals**, **A/B testing**, and **trigger testing** before looking at how skills are stored, maintained, and shared.

4

Testing, Maintaining, and Sharing Skills

Once a skill has been created and used successfully, the next question is how thoroughly it needs to be tested. For a personal task such as drafting a LinkedIn post, an imperfect result is rarely a serious problem. The stakes change when a skill produces invoices, financial models, or any material that will be shared outside the organization. In those cases, we need a way to confirm that the skill performs as expected and follows every rule defined within it.

Claude provides three ways to test a skill, and none of them requires writing code. Each method is driven by an ordinary request to the built-in **Skill Creator**. **Evals** check whether a skill follows objective requirements, **A/B testing** compares the quality of two versions, and **trigger testing** checks whether the skill activates at the right moment. Used together, these methods form a quality loop: we test the skill, find where it falls short, ask Claude to revise it, and save the improved version.

Testing is only part of making a skill dependable. We also need to understand where skills are stored, how a **hosted skill** differs from a **local skill**, and which sharing route suits an individual, a team, or a whole organization. The chapter closes with a more sophisticated example: a *pre-call briefing skill* that shows how a single focused skill can pull information from several connected tools and produce more than one polished output.

In this chapter, we will cover the following topics:

- Understanding the skill quality loop
- Running evals
- Comparing skill versions with A/B testing
- Testing trigger behavior

- Maintaining and storing skills
- Sharing skills
- Examining a sophisticated skill

Technical requirements

To follow the testing examples in this chapter, you will need the following:

- A Claude account with access to **Skills** and the built-in **Skill Creator**
- At least one existing skill that can be tested
- Access to **Claude Chat** or **Claude Cowork**

The local-storage discussion uses **Claude Cowork**, because Cowork is the interface that can work with folders on your computer. The pre-call briefing example also relies on connected services such as **Google Calendar**, **HubSpot**, **Gmail**, a call-recording tool, **LinkedIn**, and **web browsing**. Those services support that particular workflow, but they are not required to understand the testing methods themselves.

No programming knowledge is required. Every testing method begins by asking Claude to use a *capability* that is already built into Skill Creator.

Understanding the skill quality loop

How much testing a **skill** needs depends on the cost of getting the output wrong. A personal skill used to draft a post or explore an idea may never need formal evaluation. A skill that prepares invoices, calculates financial figures, creates customer-facing material, or produces anything that leaves the organization deserves more deliberate checking.

The question a skill must answer is always the same: is it performing as expected and following all the rules defined inside it? Visual quality alone does not settle that question. An invoice can look polished while carrying the wrong bank details, the wrong tax number, or an incorrect currency conversion. A presentation can appear professional while quietly breaking one of the brand rules it is supposed to enforce.

Claude offers three ways to examine these different dimensions of **quality**:

- **Evals** are the objective test. They ask whether the required elements are present and correct.
- **A/B testing** is a comparative test. It asks which of two outputs is stronger.
- **Trigger testing** is the behavioral test; it asks whether Claude recognized that the skill was relevant in the first place.

Figure 4.1 summarizes the three testing approaches and the question each answers.

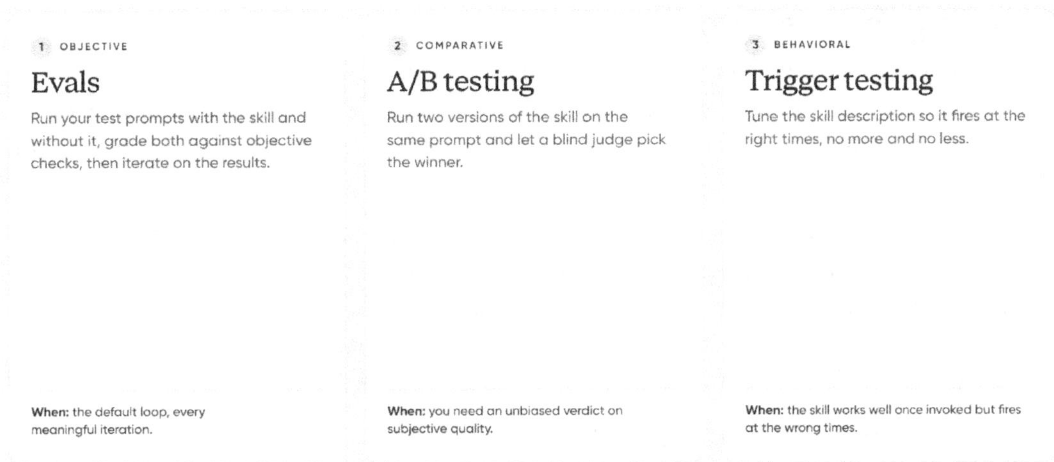

Figure 4.1: Evals, A/B testing, and trigger testing examine objective compliance, comparative quality, and activation behavior

These methods answer different questions, so they complement one another rather than replace one another. A skill can pass one test and still need work in the area another test measures. All three are capabilities inside Skill Creator, which is a built-in skill available in every Claude account, so there is no separate testing tool to install and no code to write. We only need to tell Claude which skill to test and which method to use.

Running evals

An *eval* is an evaluation of a skill. It runs the skill against realistic prompts and compares the results with the requirements written into the body of the skill. The goal is not to understand evaluation systems in any technical depth; it is to get a practical answer to a direct question: does this skill follow the rules we gave it?

The process starts with a request such as:

```
Use the skill creator skill to run evals on my invoice creator skill.
```

The same pattern works for a **presentation skill**, a **reporting skill**, or any other skill whose output can be checked against objective requirements. If the skill has just been created, the request can be made in the same conversation, for example, `Run evals on this skill`. Skill Creator reads the skill, works out which rules should be tested, and generates likely prompts that would activate it. In the invoice example, Skill Creator generates three prompts.

Choosing the test prompts

There are two ways to define the prompts an **evaluation (eval)** uses. We can supply the scenarios ourselves, or we can let Claude generate them from the skill. When Claude generates the prompts, it presents them for review so they can be accepted, edited, or added to before the evaluation begins.

I recommend letting Claude create the scenarios in most cases. Because Skill Creator can read the entire skill, it already understands the process, the intended triggers, and the rules that need to be exercised. Defining every scenario by hand is possible, but it usually makes the evaluation more complicated without a clear benefit. The important point is that the prompts should represent different situations in which the *skill* is expected to do its job.

Running the skill and baseline

Each test prompt is run twice, once with the skill and once without it. The run without the skill is the **baseline**. It shows what Claude would produce from the same request without the specialized instructions, examples, assets, and rules the skill contains.

Three approved prompts therefore create six runs: prompt one with and without the skill, then the same pairing for prompts two and three. The runs take place in separate contexts that do not communicate with one another, so the output or instructions from one scenario cannot influence another. Keeping the contexts separate is what makes the comparison meaningful, because we see how the skill behaves across genuinely independent scenarios rather than inside one long conversation where earlier results color later ones. The following figure shows the three prompts being run with and without the skill as six separate tasks.

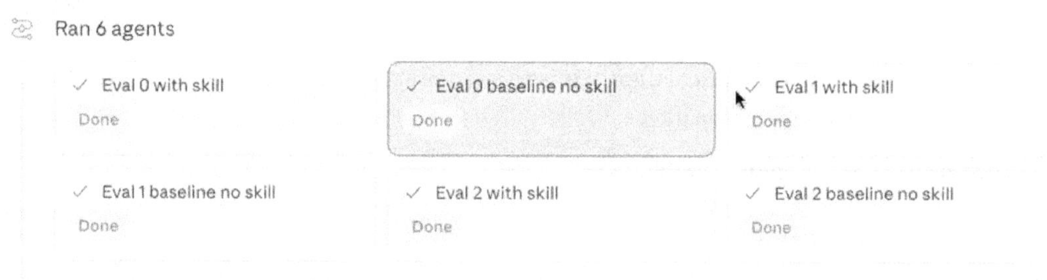

Figure 4.2: Skill Creator runs each of the three test prompts with and without the skill

Reviewing the outputs and benchmark

Skill Creator provides a viewer that pairs each prompt with the output it produced. Each page shows the prompt alongside the output that prompt generated, and moving to the next result steps from the run with the skill to the same prompt run without it, so we can inspect the skill-enabled output beside the baseline.

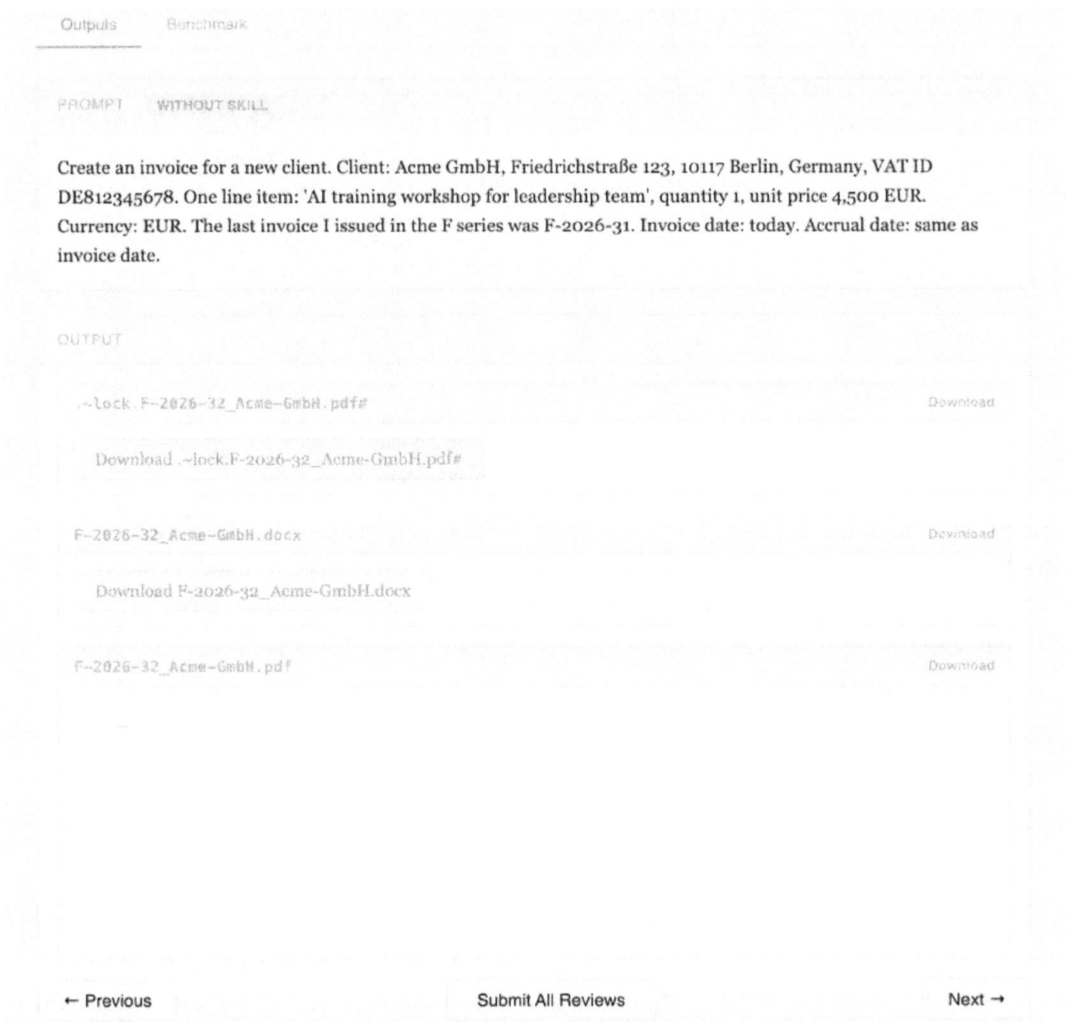

Figure 4.3: The Eval Review viewer for the notlinear-invoice skill displays a test prompt alongside the files generated for the run without the skill

In the invoice comparison, the difference is immediately visible: the invoice created with the skill follows the company brand, logo, and layout, while the baseline invoice reflects none of them.

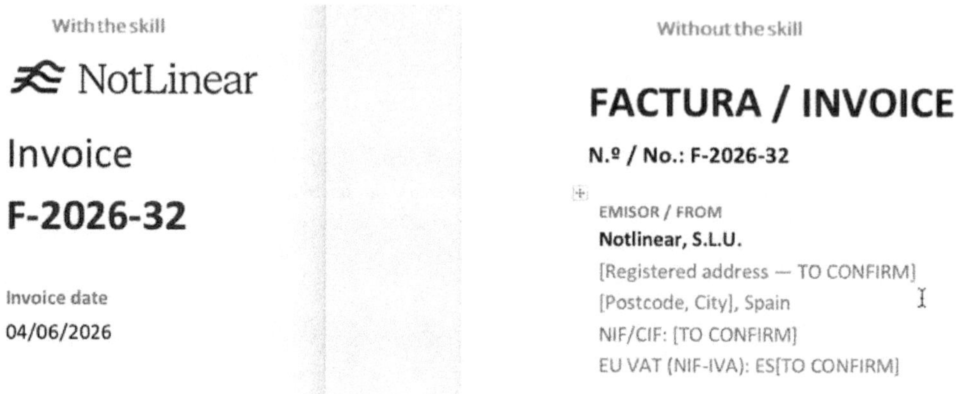

Figure 4.4: The skill-enabled invoice follows the required branding and layout, while the baseline output retains generic formatting and unresolved placeholders

This visual comparison is useful, but the most important part of an eval is the **benchmark**. The benchmark reports which objective checks each run passed and which it failed. Skill Creator reads the body of the skill and turns its requirements into checks. For the invoice skill, those checks include details such as:

- Invoice number
- Required IBAN
- USD exchange rate
- VAT number
- Tax number
- Expected branding and formatting

In this eval, the run with the skill follows every rule and reaches 100 percent accuracy, while the baseline misses many of them. The benchmark can also compare pass rate, execution time, token cost, and the differences between the skill-enabled output and the baseline. This confirms that the skill is doing more than producing an attractive document; it is teaching Claude to perform the task according to the operational details that matter.

ASSERTION	WITH SKILL	WITHOUT SKILL
Invoice number F-2026-32 appears in the document	✓	✓
Correct IBAN [illegible] present	✓	✗
Legacy IBAN from old Pietro Montaldo invoices absent	✓	✓
EUR bank block present ([illegible])	✓	✗
USD-only bank lines absent (no correspondent BIC [illegible] on EUR invoice)	✓	✓
Article 69 reverse-charge footer present (EU client outside Spain)	✓	✓
Total-only layout: no IVA/VAT amount line rendered	✓	✓
Issuer EU VAT [illegible] on the invoice	✓	✗
No unresolved placeholders in the document	✓	✗
Client VAT ID [illegible] present	✓	✓
Total of 4,500.00 rendered	✓	✓
Two-pass flow respected: no PDF generated before user approval	✓	✗
Filename is 2026-06-04-invoice-F-2026-32.docx (generation-date convention)	✓	✗

Figure 4.5: The benchmark compares the skill-enabled and baseline outputs against each objective requirement

Improving the skill from the eval

The same benchmark can reveal a weaker result. A first or lightly tested skill may fail several checks because it is too long, an instruction is unclear, or one requirement is easy to overlook. Those failures are not a reason to abandon the skill; they are a precise starting point for improving it. Running evals on a skill that has not yet been refined extensively will almost always surface rules that are not being followed.

Once the results are reviewed, Claude can be asked to fix the failures directly, for example, `Based on the eval results, some of the rules were not followed. Help me fix the skill so that it meets those requirements.` Claude inspects the failed checks, revises the skill, and runs the evaluation again as a new iteration. The loop continues until the skill performs at the required level:

1. Run the test prompts.
2. Compare the skill output with the baseline.
3. Review the objective checks.
4. Identify the failed requirements.

5. Revise the skill.
6. Run the evaluation again.

Because the benchmark also reports time and token cost, we can see whether an improved skill follows more rules while also changing the resources the task requires. Output quality remains the priority, but those extra measurements help reveal the effect of each iteration. Evals are the default testing loop for any skill whose quality can be judged objectively, and they are especially useful after a meaningful change, because they show whether the revision solved the intended problem without pulling the skill away from its other rules.

Comparing skill versions with A/B testing

Evals grade a skill and its baseline against objective checks. A/B testing answers a different question: which of two skill versions produces the better result?

This becomes more useful as a skill matures. A new iteration may look stronger, but the difference can be hard to judge by reading the instructions alone. **A/B testing** runs the same prompt through both versions and lets an independent judge compare the outputs without being told which version produced which. A request follows this pattern:

```
Use the skill creator skill to A/B test two versions of my brand skill, version A
versus version B.
```

The two versions being compared might be:

- The current skill and a proposed revision
- A **personal skill** and an externally created skill
- The same skill run with two different models
- Two approaches to the same creative workflow

Figure 4.6 summarizes how two skill versions are compared through a blind judgment.

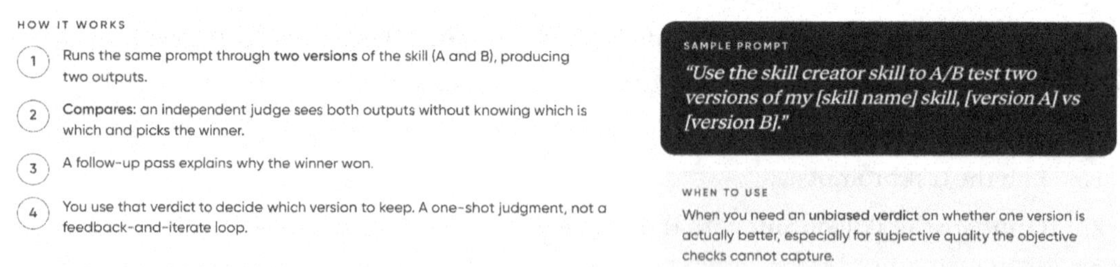

Figure 4.6: The same prompt is run through two skill versions before a blind judge selects the stronger output and explains the decision

To demonstrate A/B testing, I compare my NotLinear brand skill with **Anthropic's Brand Guidelines Skill**. Both skills receive the same request. The output from my skill reflects the established NotLinear visual identity, while the more general Anthropic skill is less specific and resembles a standard landing page. The comparison shows where each skill follows the intended rules and where it does not.

The comparison also reveals that the preferred skill failed to follow one of its own rules. This shows that A/B testing and evals are not mutually exclusive: one output can be judged better overall while still containing an objective failure that needs correcting. When such a failure appears, the skill can be revised in the same way as after an eval; for example, `Review the comparison and help me fix the rule that was not followed.`

A/B testing is particularly valuable when the difference between outputs is subjective, because brand voice, creative direction, and writing style cannot always be reduced to a list of binary checks. LinkedIn content is a good example: a skill might help write hooks, review a draft, or strengthen part of a post, and two results can both meet the stated requirements while differing in quality or in how well they match the author's voice. A blind comparison gives an unbiased judgment about which version is moving in the stronger direction. The same approach helps when a model changes, since a skill that performed well with one model may behave differently with another. Unlike the iterative loop used for evals, A/B testing delivers a one-shot comparative verdict: it identifies which version performs better and explains why, so we can decide which one to keep.

Testing trigger behavior

A skill can produce excellent output once it is running and still fail in everyday use if it activates at the wrong time. Every skill carries a description, and that description tells Claude when the skill should trigger. Because skills are portable and can become relevant in any conversation, the description has to separate requests that genuinely need the skill from requests that merely mention a related topic.

Trigger testing measures that behavior. It is the method to reach for when a skill does not activate when it should, activates when it should stay inactive, or needs repeated manual prompting before Claude recognizes it. The process begins with a request such as:

```
Use the skill creator skill to test the trigger quality of my invoice skill.
```

Skill Creator reads the skill description and generates a test set. In the invoice example, the set contains ten prompts that should trigger the skill and ten that should not. The prompts can be reviewed, edited, or supplemented before the test runs. Because triggering is probabilistic, each query is run several times rather than judged on a single result, and the results are measured on a held-out test set so the chosen description is not tuned only to the original examples. The following figure summarizes how trigger queries are tested and how the skill description is refined.

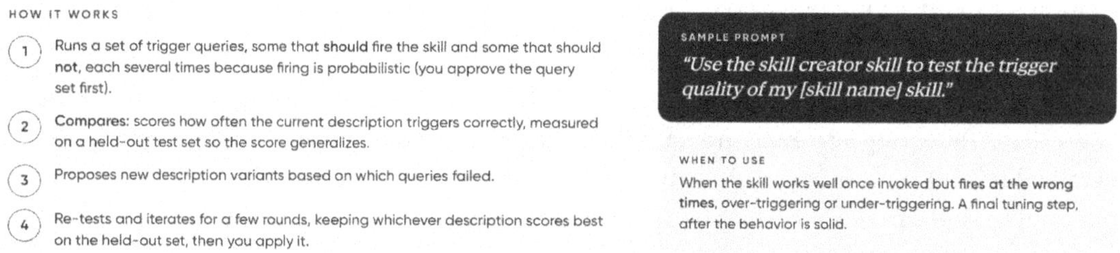

Figure 4.7: Trigger testing measures positive and negative queries, proposes revised descriptions, and retains the strongest version

The positive prompts express an intent that requires the skill, such as asking Claude to generate, prepare, or create an invoice. The negative prompts may contain the word invoice without asking for one to be created, such as a general question about an existing invoice. In this test, two negative prompts incorrectly activate the skill because Claude interprets the mention of an invoice as a request to begin the invoice creation process.

This kind of false positive wastes time and credits, because Claude begins a workflow that does not match the request. A false negative causes the opposite problem: the workflow exists, but Claude does not recognize that the request matches it, so the user has to add instructions or search for the skill manually. Both failures point to a description that needs refinement.

After reviewing the failed queries, Claude can be asked to revise the description, for example, `Review these trigger-test failures. The skill activated twice when it should not have. Adjust the description so that this does not happen again.` Skill Creator proposes alternative descriptions based on the queries that failed, tests them for several rounds, and keeps whichever version scores best on the held-out set. Once the description is improved, Claude returns an updated skill, and that update must be saved. If it is not saved, Claude keeps using the earlier description and the trigger failures remain.

The wider point is that *skills are invoked through intent*. A skill can be selected manually or with a slash command, but that should not be necessary for ordinary use. A well-written description lets Claude recognize the task from natural language, so we do not have to memorize skill names. That matters more as the number of skills grows, because searching a long list defeats much of the value of reusable skills. When Claude fails to recognize the intent, trigger testing gives us a way to improve the description rather than settling for a permanent manual workaround.

This is why the description matters more than the name. Even a skill with an unrelated name can trigger correctly for invoice work when its description clearly matches the user's intent.

Maintaining and storing skills

Testing shows what needs to change, but the improved version only becomes useful when it is maintained and stored correctly. Before comparing storage locations, there is one rule that applies to every revision: ***always save the skill after creating or updating it***. A change made inside a conversation does not automatically replace the version stored in your account. If the updated skill is not saved, later conversations continue using the old version. This is true for the first creation and for every later edit.

Letting a skill improve as it is used

Two optional rules can help a skill improve over time. The first turns negative feedback into a new rule. When the user tells the skill to stop doing something, the skill can update its own rules so the correction is remembered. A line inside `SKILL.md` might read:

```
Add a progressive update rule: when the user specifies something not to do
anymore, update this skill's rules section so the behavior is never repeated.
```

The second rule turns successful output into examples. After a result has been approved, the final version can be stored so future runs have another concrete example of what good work looks like:

```
After every approved output, save the final result as a new example file inside
references/examples/ so future runs can reference it.
```

Figure 4.8 brings these two improvement patterns together.

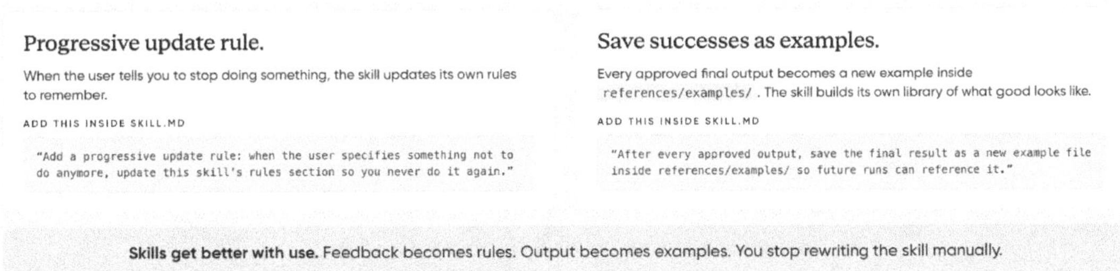

Figure 4.8: Negative feedback can become a new rule, while approved output can be stored as a future example

Treat these as advanced additions rather than a complete self-maintaining system. Their role is straightforward: feedback becomes rules, and approved output becomes examples. The resulting changes still need to be reviewed and saved so the account uses the intended version.

Hosted skills

A hosted skill lives in your Claude account, or in an organization's skill environment, and is reached through the **Customize** section. Hosted skills synchronize across every device where the same account is used, remain available outside the conversation or computer where they were created, are easier to share with a team, and receive updates through the account. This is where skills should normally live, because saving a skill to the account keeps it available whether work continues in **Chat**, **Cowork**, a browser, or on another computer.

Hosted updates can also change how a skill behaves. When a skill is maintained by another party or distributed through an organization, an update may be applied without any file on your machine changing. ***It is worth checking the changelog before relying on an updated hosted skill for an important workflow***.

Local skills

Cowork always works inside a folder on your computer. When a *local skill* is created while Cowork is working in that folder, Claude may save the skill locally if the account-level save is not completed. A local skill exists only on that computer, is available only when Cowork is working in the relevant folder, does not synchronize to other devices, must be updated by hand, and can be shared only by sending or copying the file. The following figure compares the practical consequences of hosting a skill in Claude and keeping it locally.

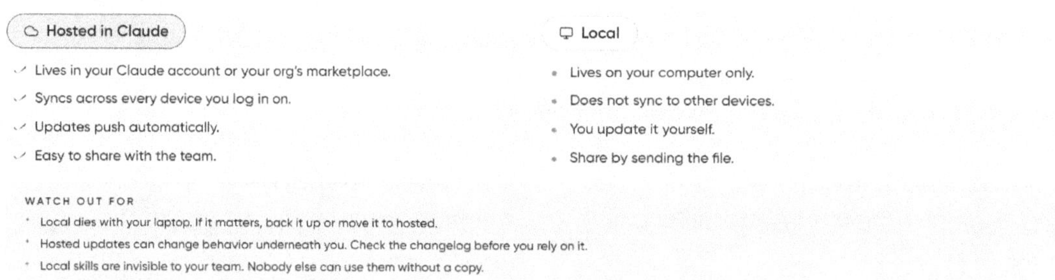

Figure 4.9: The hosted-versus-local comparison, showing account synchronization, device availability, update behavior, and sharing for each storage location

A local skill can therefore appear to work during the original Cowork task yet be unavailable from another conversation, interface, folder, or device. It also carries a backup risk: if the computer or folder is lost, the skill is lost with it, and it stays invisible to the rest of the team unless someone distributes a copy manually. The practical recommendation is to save important skills into **Customize** regardless of whether they were created in Chat or Cowork. Local storage can support a particular working folder, but hosted storage makes the skill available across the account.

Sharing skills

The right sharing method depends on the account type, the number of recipients, and whether updates need to be distributed centrally. There are four routes for sharing a single skill:

- **Organization-wide distribution.** An organization administrator can install a skill across the workspace so that every relevant member receives it automatically. A team lead can be granted skill-administration access to distribute approved skills through the company account. This is the most centralized route, because individual users do not need to download or reinstall anything.
- **Sharing inside a Claude Team plan.** Members of the same Team or Enterprise environment can share a skill directly through the Claude interface by opening the **share** option and choosing the colleague with whom to share it. This native route is preferable to downloading a file and asking someone to install it manually.
- **Sharing through a Drive folder.** A `skill` folder can be placed in a shared Drive location, from which team members copy or install it locally. This works, but each user must fetch the revised files whenever the skill changes, so it provides access without automatic distribution.
- **Sending an individual file.** When native team sharing is not available, the skill can be exported as a `.md` or `.skill` file and sent by email, Slack, or another tool, after which the recipient installs it manually. This suits one-off sharing but is less convenient when the skill changes often.

These four routes are meant for sharing a single skill. When several related skills need to travel together, a *plugin* is the better option, because it can package multiple skills and their capabilities into one unit. We will not develop plugin creation in detail here, but the distinction is useful: share an individual skill when one focused workflow is needed, and consider a plugin when several skills need to operate together. Whatever route is used, every revision must be saved before it is distributed, because sending an old file or sharing an unsaved version leaves other users with the behavior the testing process was meant to replace.

Examining a sophisticated skill

A skill should do one job, but that does not mean it can draw on only one source. A single focused objective may require information from several systems, some research, approved examples, and more than one output format. The *pre-call briefing skill* illustrates this balance.

Its job is to research the external people involved in an upcoming call and prepare a polished, on-brand briefing, which is useful in sales, company leadership, or any role that involves frequent meetings with customers, partners, or other stakeholders.

The skill does not try to manage the entire relationship or perform every sales activity. It has one outcome, preparing the user for the call, and to reach it, the skill coordinates information from across the technology stack. The process can instruct Claude to check the calendar for the meeting and its participants, review earlier email exchanges, review previous call recordings, read relationship and deal information from the CRM, research the participant on Apollo and LinkedIn, and carry out additional web research, all while using approved branding and output examples. *Figure 4.10* maps the sources and outputs involved in the pre-call briefing workflow.

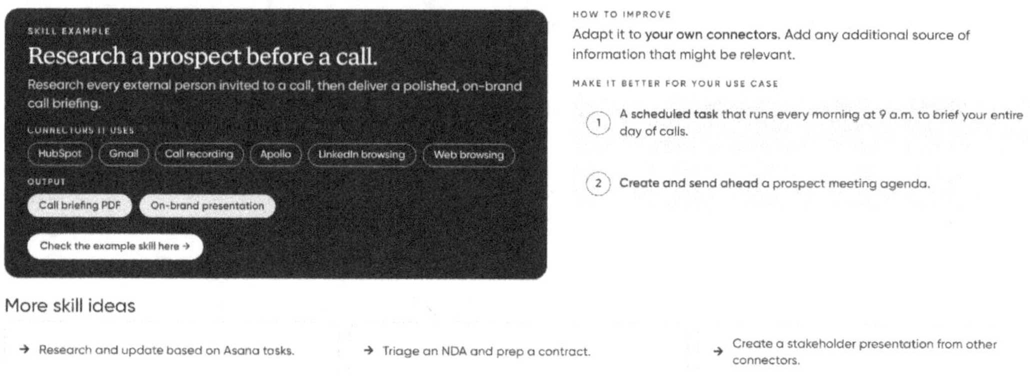

Figure 4.10: The pre-call briefing skill, showing its connections to HubSpot, Gmail, call recordings, Apollo, LinkedIn browsing, and web browsing, together with its PDF and presentation outputs

The workflow begins with a request to run the skill for a particular account, such as `Run the pre-call brief skill on this account`. Claude loads the skill and reads the sources available through the connected environment, and the context area shows Google Calendar, HubSpot, Gmail, the Fathom call recorder, and Web research being used.

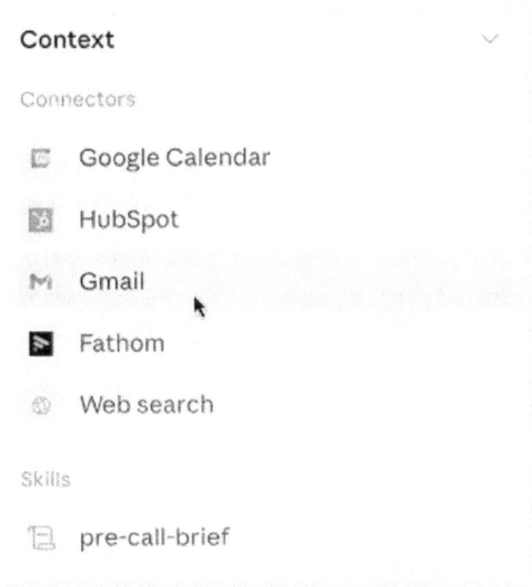

Figure 4.11: The Cowork Context panel shows the connectors used by the pre-call-brief skill, including Google Calendar, HubSpot, Gmail, Fathom, and web search

Where a connector allows it, Claude can also write information back into the technology stack, so the output could be a file, a presentation, or an email draft, depending on how the process is designed.

The workflow generates both a PDF briefing and an HTML presentation. The PDF includes the company and participant roles, the objective of the call, the company profile, the value of the deal, the people included in the meeting, relationship history drawn from the CRM and email exchanges, talking points based on recent communication, shared interests or common ground, risks and landmines, and smart questions to ask. The same research is then transformed into a presentation that can be used for internal preparation, a discussion with a manager, or a meeting with an investor or other stakeholder. The connectors provide access to the information, while the skill defines how the research is performed and how the final briefing is organized.

The *pre-call skill* can be adapted to the connectors and sources available in another environment, and further sources can be added when they contribute to the preparation. Two useful extensions are scheduling the skill to run every morning at 9 a.m. to prepare briefings for the whole day of calls, and creating and sending a meeting agenda to the prospect before the call. The same pattern suits other focused outcomes as well, such as researching and updating work based on **Asana** tasks, triaging an NDA and preparing a contract, or building a stakeholder presentation from connected sources.

The point is not that every workflow should become as elaborate as this one. The example shows how much research and coordination a single skill can perform while still serving one defined job. The 500-line recommendation discussed earlier provides a practical upper boundary. If the briefing skill grows too long, divide the process into two focused skills and chain them so that the output of the first becomes the input of the second. This preserves the complete workflow without forcing every instruction into one oversized skill.

Once a skill has been tested and refined, using it can become very simple: we provide the request, Claude follows the stored process, and the required output is returned. In the next chapter, we will extend this model by examining how **connectors** give skills access to external tools and how **subagents** handle repeated or context-heavy work.

Summary

In this chapter, we established a quality loop for skills whose outputs need to be dependable. Evals compare a skill-enabled result with a baseline and grade both against objective checks; the invoice example showed how the benchmark can verify the invoice number, the IBAN, the USD exchange rate, the VAT and tax numbers, and the required branding before a skill is used for important work. A/B testing then compares two skill versions through a blind judgment, which is useful when **quality is subjective**, when a new iteration must be weighed against an earlier one, or when the same skill is tested across different models. Trigger testing addressed the behavioral side of reliability by exposing false positives and false negatives and improving the description Claude uses to recognize intent.

We saw that maintenance continues after testing: feedback can become new rules, approved outputs can become examples, and every revision must be saved so the updated version becomes the one the account uses. Hosted skills synchronize across devices and are easier to share, while **local Cowork skills** stay tied to one computer and folder unless they are backed up or moved into hosted storage. We also examined four routes for sharing a single skill, namely organization-wide distribution, native sharing inside a Team plan, a shared Drive folder, and an individual `.md` or `.skill` file, and noted that a **plugin** is the better option when several skills need to travel together.

Finally, the pre-call briefing skill showed how one focused workflow can coordinate calendars, email, CRM records, call recordings, LinkedIn, and web research to produce a detailed PDF and an on-brand presentation, and how it can be extended through scheduling or additional outputs or split into focused skills when it grows too long. The next chapter builds on this foundation by examining the systems that give skills access to external tools, beginning with **connectors** and **Model Context Protocol** (**MCP**) before exploring how subagents divide repeated, context-heavy work.

5

Extending Skills with Connectors and Subagents

A skill teaches Claude how to perform a task, but most real tasks depend on information that already lives somewhere else. Customer details sit in a **CRM**, work items sit in a task manager such as **Asana**, payment data sits in **Stripe**, meetings sit in a calendar, and previous exchanges sit in email or a call-recording tool. Without a way to reach those systems, that information has to be copied into the conversation by hand every time. **Connectors** remove that step: once an external service is connected, Claude can read from it and often write back to it, while the skill defines what to do with the information it finds.

Some work is also too heavy, too repetitive, or too context-hungry to sit comfortably inside a single conversation. Reading forty articles, researching a long list of leads, or running several independent checks at once can fill the main chat with intermediate detail that crowds out everything else. **Subagents** address this by letting Claude hand parts of the work to separate copies of itself, each working in its own context and returning only the useful result. The three capabilities are complementary: connectors provide access to external information, skills provide the process, and subagents provide a way to organize demanding work.

We will begin with connectors and the **Model Context Protocol (MCP)** behind them, then examine the most efficient ways for Claude to reach external tools and build repeatable skills around that access. The second half of the chapter turns to subagents and the role they can play in demanding skill-based workflows in Cowork.

In this chapter, we will cover the following topics:

- Connecting Claude to external tools
- Understanding MCP and connectors
- Choosing how Claude reaches external tools

- Building skills on top of connectors
- Understanding subagents
- Using subagents inside a skill
- Understanding subagent limitations

Technical requirements

To follow the concepts and interface examples in this chapter, you will need the following:

- A Claude account with access to **Skills**
- Access to the **Customize** section in **Claude Chat** or **Claude Cowork**
- Claude Cowork, which is required for browser control and subagents
- An account for any external service you want to connect, such as a CRM, Asana, Stripe, or a call-recording tool

Connector availability can depend on the account and on the policies an organization applies. In a managed Team or Enterprise environment, only approved connectors may appear, whereas an individual account or an organization administrator may have access to a broader connector catalog. No programming background is required. This chapter explains MCP only at the level needed to understand how Claude communicates with external tools; building an MCP server yourself is outside the scope of this book.

Connecting Claude to external tools

Most organizations already keep their important information inside a technology stack. **Customer records** may live in a CRM such as HubSpot or Salesforce, **tasks** in Asana, **payments** in Stripe, **meetings** in a calendar, and earlier conversations in **email** or a **call-recording service**. Without a connector, that information has to be moved manually: you open HubSpot, copy the customer record, return to Claude, paste it into the conversation, and only then ask Claude to use it.

A connector changes that relationship. Once the external service is connected, Claude reaches the information directly through the Claude interface. Instead of copying a record into the chat, the workflow can ask Claude to retrieve the relevant account, read what is available, and use it as part of the task.

Browsing and adding a connector

Connectors are managed from the **Customize** section in Claude. The general process is:

1. Open **Customize** from Claude Chat or Claude Cowork.
2. Open the **Connectors** section.

3. Choose the option to browse connectors.
4. Find the service you need.
5. Add the connector.
6. Sign in to the external account when prompted.

Figure 5.1 shows the connector directory available through **Customize**.

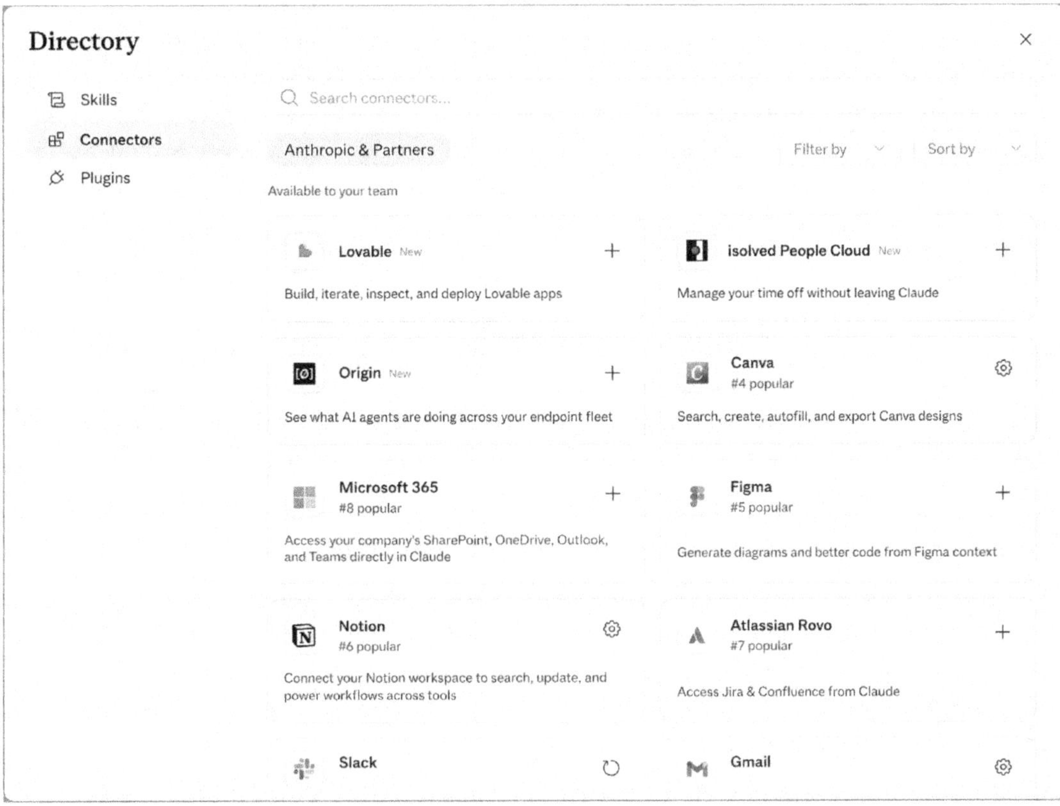

Figure 5.1: The Connectors directory in Customize, where available integrations can be searched and installed

After you add a connector, Claude prompts you to sign in to the external tool with your credentials.

Once authentication is complete, Claude can work with the connected service according to the access that service grants. For an Asana connector, that may mean reviewing existing tasks, creating a new task, or using task information to prepare a report. A CRM connector may allow Claude to read account information and, where the integration supports it, write an update back to the record.

The catalog you see can differ by environment. In an organization-managed account, administrators may decide which external services can be connected, which lets the organization control access to **customer**, **financial**, and **operational systems**. In an individual account, the available catalog is usually less restricted. In a large organization, custom or external connectors may be restricted, leaving only pre-vetted integrations available.

Working with live information instead of copying it

Connecting a tool reduces how much information has to be stored separately inside Claude. Consider a sales workflow where every account already exists in a CRM. Rather than building a project that duplicates those records, Claude can connect to the CRM and retrieve the current information whenever the workflow runs. Copying the same data into a project would create a second version that can drift out of date, whereas the connector lets Claude work with the information where it already lives.

This does not make projects redundant. A project still holds static material that does not live in a connected system: internal guidance, research files, contracts, and other reference documents. The connector and the project serve different purposes. The connector provides access to live external systems, while the project holds supporting material those systems do not contain. A connected workflow may therefore combine live account details from a CRM, meetings from a calendar, earlier exchanges from email, call history from a recording service, and static reference material from a project.

Reading from and writing to connected tools

Connectors are not limited to retrieving information. Depending on the service and the permissions granted, Claude can also write information back. Claude might read a set of Asana tasks, reason across them, and prepare a dashboard, and it might then create a new task in Asana from a request made inside Claude. A similar workflow could read an account from **HubSpot** and add a task or note to that account.

This changes what a good result looks like. The outcome is no longer only a reply inside the conversation; it can be an action completed inside the technology stack. The final objective is that Claude performs the work at the level you would expect from a capable member of the team, not merely that it describes how the work should be done.

Understanding MCP and connectors

The terms *MCP* and *connector* are often used together, but they describe different parts of the same relationship. Model Context Protocol, or MCP, is the standard through which Claude communicates with outside tools. A connector is a packaged MCP integration that can be installed inside Claude with little setup.

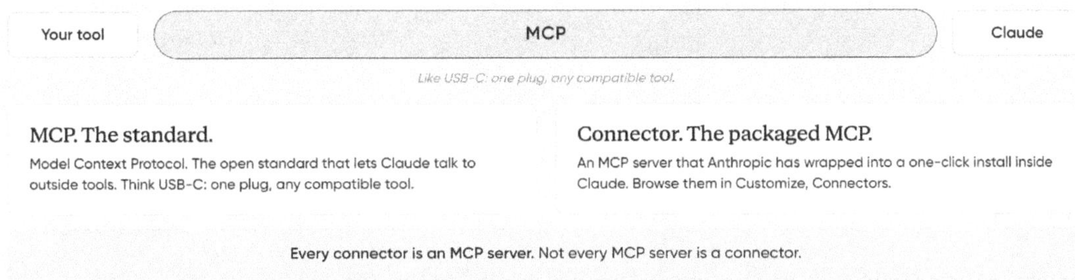

Figure 5.2: The relationship between MCP and connectors

A useful way to understand MCP is through the *USB-C analogy*. Many different devices can communicate over the same physical connection because USB-C is a shared standard. MCP provides a comparable standard for Claude and compatible external tools: one open protocol that lets any tool built for it talk to Claude. The external service holds information or capabilities that Claude does not have on its own, and MCP is the channel that translates the interaction into a form both sides understand. A CRM, a task manager, a design platform, or an internal company tool can each expose selected information and actions to Claude through an MCP server.

A connector is simply an MCP server that Anthropic has wrapped into a one-click install inside Claude, which you can browse from **Customize** under **Connectors**. The relationship can be summarized in one rule:

Every connector is an MCP server, but not every MCP server is a connector.

An external company can build an MCP server without publishing it through Claude's connector catalog. In that case, the MCP may require a separate installation process. Packaged connectors provide the simpler route because the integration has already been prepared for installation through the interface.

Choosing how Claude reaches external tools

Claude can reach an external tool in five different ways. The five levels move from direct, efficient integrations toward slower and more expensive interface-based interactions.

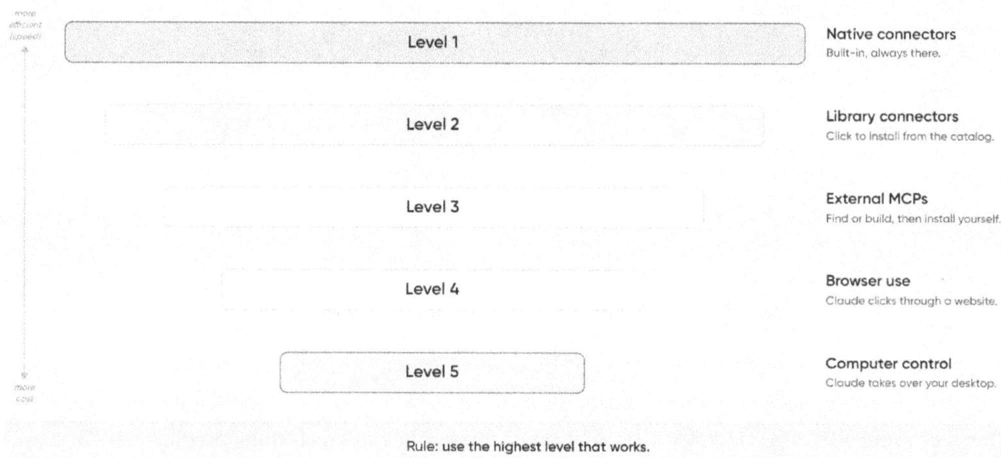

Figure 5.3: The five levels through which Claude can reach external tools

As you move down the list, speed decreases and cost increases, so the guiding rule is to use the highest level that can complete the task.

- **Level 1: Native connectors**. These are built into the Claude environment and are pre-installed in every account, so they need no separate setup. **Excel** is an example of a native connector: Claude can work with Excel through this native capability without your having to find or install anything. Because the connection is direct, it is the fastest and cheapest option.
- **Level 2: Library connectors**. These are packaged in the connector catalog and can be added through **Customize** in a few steps. In a managed environment, the catalog may contain only the services the organization has reviewed and approved. This level is convenient because you do not have to find, configure, or build the MCP server yourself.
- **Level 3: External MCPs**. Some tools provide their own MCP server outside Claude's catalog, and these must be found and installed separately. **Tella**'s MCP is an example of an external MCP that may need to be installed from the provider's website rather than through Claude's connector catalog. This can open up a service that is not available as a packaged connector, but large organizations often prevent employees from installing external MCPs for security or compliance reasons, so Level 3 may be unavailable there.
- **Level 4: Browser use**. When no connector or external MCP is available, Claude can control the browser to read what appears on screen and act through the website's interface. This is the same mechanism used in the Custom GPT migration method described in *Chapter 2*, where Claude takes control of the browser, opens **ChatGPT**, and

reads the Custom GPTs or projects there in order to build a skill. Because Claude may need to inspect the page, select an element, scroll, and inspect the next view, browser use is slower and more expensive than a direct integration. It works by taking a screenshot, interpreting it, and acting on the next view, but it remains a useful fallback.

- **Level 5: Computer control**. *Computer control* extends the same idea beyond a single web page: Claude operates the desktop and interacts with applications through their interfaces. It is the least efficient and most costly level because the work depends on visual interpretation and repeated interface actions, so it is reserved for tasks that none of the higher levels can perform.

The order of preference is therefore native connector, then library connector, then external MCP, then browser use, and finally computer control. The recommendation is not to reach for browser control simply because it can imitate the way a person clicks through a screen. The first question is always whether a native or packaged integration already exists; browser use and computer control are fallbacks for when it does not.

A practical starting point is to identify the five tools you use most in your day-to-day work and check which of them are available through Anthropic's connector catalog. These may include **Google Drive**, email, calendar, a CRM, task management, or payment processing. The aim is not to connect everything without a plan, but to ask what work you repeatedly perform inside each service. Those repeated processes become the starting point for a skill.

Building skills on top of connectors

A connector provides access, but access alone does not make a useful workflow. Claude may be able to open a **Canva** presentation, retrieve Stripe transactions, or read a call transcript, yet it still needs instructions explaining what to do with that information. The connector gives Claude access to the tool; the skill teaches Claude how to use that access for a particular task. Anything you do repeatedly with a connector should be codified into a skill. Other possibilities include using an **Excalidraw** connector to create visual diagrams and using call recordings as the basis for a weekly sales-coaching skill.

Proofreading Canva presentations

Consider a presentation built in Canva. The final stage often involves checking spelling and typographical errors, spacing, brand consistency, and any language that should not appear, along with other presentation-specific rules. The **Canva connector** gives Claude access to the deck, while a proofreading skill defines the checks to run and the standards to apply. You point Claude to the Canva deck, ask it to run the proofreading process, and Claude loads the skill, examines the deck through the connector, and reviews it against the rules you have set.

The value extends beyond finding problems. After Claude reports its findings, you review the proposed corrections, and if you approve them and the connector provides write access, Claude returns to the design tool and applies them directly. The process therefore contains a natural human-in-the-loop checkpoint: Claude reviews the deck, reports the issues, you review the proposed changes, and approved changes are applied through the connector. Final proofreading suits a skill well because it is repetitive and follows defined rules, and it does not need the same creative judgment as designing the presentation in the first place.

Preparing Stripe reports

Stripe offers a second example. At the end of each month, payment information may need to be reviewed so that transactions can be reconciled and the results prepared for an accountant or a tax process. The **Stripe connector** provides access to the payment data, and a skill defines how that data should be retrieved, checked, reconciled, organized for tax reporting, and used to prepare invoices. Without the skill, Claude can reach the information but has no organization-specific process for using it; with the skill, the repeated accounting workflow, including the structure the accountant expects and the checks that must pass before the output is accepted, is captured once and reused every month.

Creating follow-up emails from call recordings

Call recordings provide a third example. A **recording connector** gives Claude access to the meeting transcript, and a follow-up email skill defines how to turn that conversation into a useful message: identifying the key topics discussed, the promises made during the call, any material to send, and the agreed-upon next steps. Claude then applies the format, tone, and rules held in the skill to produce the email. A request can be as simple as asking Claude to generate the follow-up email with the skill for a particular call, and Claude finds the recording through the connector, retrieves the content, and applies the skill without the transcript being copied by hand.

Combining several connectors

A skill is not limited to one connector. A single focused process can draw on several services at once. A meeting-preparation skill, for example, might use the calendar to identify the meeting, the CRM to understand the account, email to review earlier exchanges, call recordings to recall previous commitments, Asana to check open tasks, and web or LinkedIn research to gather current context. The skill defines where each type of information comes from and how the sources combine, while the connectors provide access to retrieve or update it. The relationship is not one connector to one skill: a connector can support several skills, and one skill can coordinate several connectors. What keeps the skill focused is not the number of connectors but the number of distinct jobs: every source should contribute to the same single outcome.

With the external-access layer in place, we can turn to the second extension covered in this chapter: *delegating demanding work through subagents.*

Understanding subagents

Subagents are a more advanced capability available through Claude Cowork. They are a slightly more technical topic, and if you are just getting started they may be less relevant, but it is worth knowing what they make possible. They are useful when a task contains repeated, complex, or context-heavy work that Claude can divide into separate assignments, such as processing a long list or reading a large body of material. Most everyday skill workflows can be completed without them, so subagents are best treated as a supporting capability rather than the foundation of skill creation.

The main agent and separate rooms

When you work in Claude Chat or Cowork, the current conversation acts as the main agent: it receives your request, reasons about the task, and coordinates the work. In Cowork, the main agent can create new copies of itself and assign parts of a complex task to them. A helpful way to picture this is that each subagent opens its own room. The subagent does its assigned work outside the main conversation, with fresh context and the same tools, and returns only the relevant result, which keeps the main chat clean and focused.

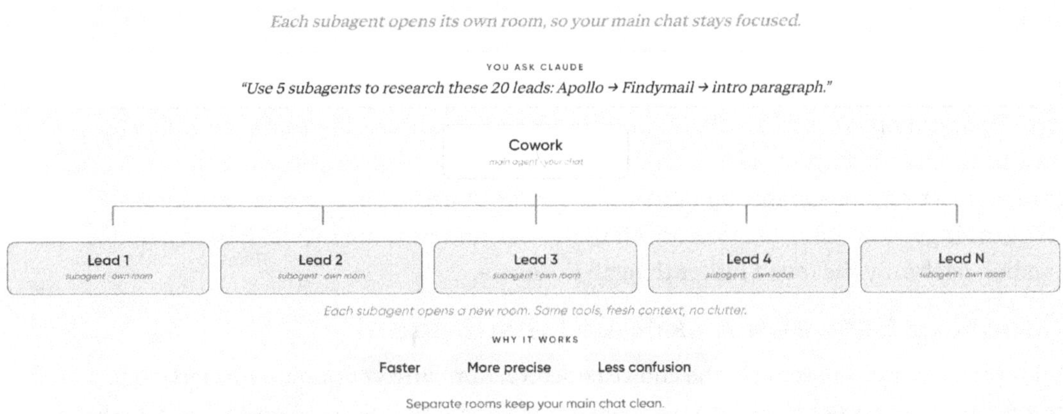

Figure 5.4: The main agent delegates parts of a lead-research workload to separate subagents, each working in its own context before reporting back

Consider a list of people to research. Instead of processing each person in turn inside the main conversation, Claude can assign different people to separate subagents. One researches the first person, another the second, and so on. The main agent then consolidates what they return. The intermediate research does not need to fill the main conversation; each subagent returns a concise result when its assignment is complete.

Comparing skills and subagents

A skill and a subagent solve different problems. A skill is a saved set of instructions that Claude follows when a task matches your request; it can hold a `SKILL.md` file together with reference files and scripts, and its process stays visible in the main workflow. A subagent is a separate copy of Claude that takes one task off to the side; it has its own window, tools, and optionally its own model, but it does not contain a permanent package of files and scripts. Put simply:

> *A skill changes how Claude works. A subagent changes who does the work and where it happens.*

CAPABILITY	SKILL	SUBAGENT
Inject a repeatable method or workflow into the conversation	Yes	No
Can bundle reference files and scripts inside it	Yes	No
Keeps all the work visible in your main chat	Yes	No
Does the heavy work off to the side, in its own space	No	Yes
Runs several jobs at the same time	No	Yes
Great for tasks that require repeated heavy work (e.g. iteration over lists)	No	Yes
Hands back only the result, not all the noise	No	Yes
Can call on the other	*Calls a subagent*	*Uses skills*
Can start another agent under it	*Not applicable*	*No, the one hard limit*

Figure 5.5: A comparison of skill and subagent capabilities

The two are complementary rather than alternatives. A skill can instruct Claude to use subagents, and a subagent can use a relevant skill while completing its assignment. A skill is good at injecting a repeatable method into a conversation and keeping the work visible; a subagent is good at doing heavy work off to the side and running several jobs in parallel, handing back only the result rather than all the noise.

Choosing between a skill and a subagent

A few practical examples make the choice concrete. Applying your house formatting to a draft, producing an invoice or report from supplied inputs, and building a slide deck in your usual template are all work for a skill: each is a fixed, repeatable method that stays visible in the main chat and produces the same shape every time. Reading forty articles to return the five key points, or searching a large folder and reasoning across all of it for a single answer, is work for a subagent: the input is large, and you want only the conclusion rather than all the reading. Researching several companies suits subagents running in parallel, because the jobs are independent and can happen at once outside the main chat. Most everyday tasks stay as skills;

subagents earn their place on repeated heavy work, such as iterating over a list of leads or researching many accounts at the same time.

Understanding the context window

The *context window* is Claude's working memory for the current conversation: it determines how much text, code, or media Claude can process at once. Every request, response, file, and piece of retrieved information adds to that working memory. As a conversation grows, more material competes for Claude's attention, and long chats become less precise because of the accumulated detail. Subagents relieve this pressure by moving heavy work outside the main context. A subagent can read a set of articles, extract the findings, and return a short conclusion, so the main conversation receives the conclusion without the complete reading process and stays focused on coordination and final reasoning.

Using subagents inside a skill

The reason subagents matter in a book about skills is that their use can be built into the skill process itself. When the relevant step is reached, the skill can direct Claude to delegate that part of the work. A research skill might define the overall method, the sources to use, the criteria for evaluating each item, and the final format, while subagents perform the repeated research. The skill remains the method; the subagents perform the assigned parts of it, each following the same steps: retrieve the required information, apply the same evaluation criteria, produce the same result structure, and return the findings to the main agent, which combines them into the final output.

Deciding how many subagents to use

Claude will sometimes decide on its own that subagents are appropriate, but it is best practice to instruct it to use them explicitly, especially when the process is being codified into a skill, so that the delegation happens consistently every time the skill runs. For a one-off task, you can name a number, as in this example:

```
Use 5 subagents to research these 20 leads: Apollo > Findymail > intro paragraph.
```

In a reusable skill, however, avoid hard-coding a fixed count. A skill that researches prospect accounts might receive ten accounts one day and fifty the next, and a fixed number of five would not suit either. A more durable instruction keeps the prompt generic and lets Claude decide:

```
Use subagents to do this specific task.
```

Claude can then choose an appropriate number based on the size and complexity of the list. The important point is that the skill consistently tells Claude to delegate the work rather than relying on Claude to infer the requirement each time.

Subagents in evaluation

The evaluation process from the earlier chapter on testing shows subagents supporting a skill workflow. Suppose an eval contains three prompts, each run once with the skill and once without it, which creates six independent tasks. Skill Creator can assign each scenario to a separate subagent so that the runs stay isolated. The subagents execute the individual tests and return their results to the main conversation, and the main agent then compares the outputs, applies the checks, and presents the benchmark. Because each run is isolated, the context of one does not affect the other.

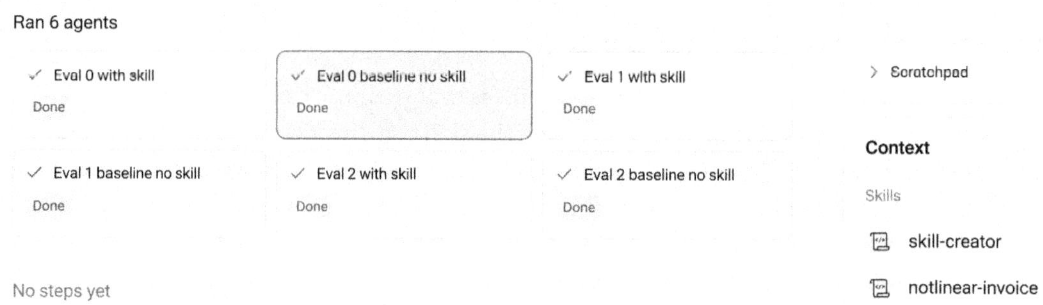

Figure 5.6: Six evaluation agents running isolated skill and baseline scenarios in Cowork

Subagents in lead intelligence

The Lead Intelligence Skill provides a second example. It assigns one subagent for every two leads, uses Apify to gather LinkedIn information, supplements it with web research, and evaluates whether each lead fits the services being offered. Each subagent returns its findings to the main agent for consolidation.

Understanding subagent limitations

Subagents improve how complex work is organized, but they are not permanent assistants that you create and manage individually. They have no persistent identity, they do not appear as named items in the **Customize** section, and there is no directory of individual agents to maintain. Claude creates the working contexts it needs as part of the task, so you do not create or manage subagents; you simply instruct Claude to use subagents for a given task, and Claude handles the delegation internally.

A useful analogy is a team lead assigning work to interns: the lead decides that parts of the task should be handled elsewhere, delegates them, and receives the results. The comparison is useful because subagents work like temporary team members, but it should not be taken literally. There is no standing research agent that must be configured before the workflow begins. The skill defines the process; the subagent is the way Claude organizes the execution of part of that process.

There is one hard limit. A subagent cannot start another subagent beneath itself. A skill can call a subagent, and a subagent can use skills, but the delegation does not continue into further layers of agents. The main agent performs the delegation and coordinates the results.

Subagents also require Cowork. Without Cowork, the same skill can still perform many ordinary tasks, but it cannot use subagent delegation. This matters when a skill is intended for an organization whose members do not yet have access to Cowork, because a required subagent step would make the whole workflow unavailable to them. A skill should therefore be designed for the interface in which it will run: a Cowork skill may include subagent delegation, browser control, and local files, while a skill meant for Claude Chat should not depend on capabilities unavailable there.

Finally, neither connectors nor subagents are required to extract value from skills. Without connectors, information can still be supplied manually or stored in a project; without subagents, repeated research can still run inside the main conversation. The process is less efficient, but the underlying skill still defines how the work should be done. A personal skill can help organize tax information, prepare recurring documents, search supplied material, or produce reports with no connectors or subagents at all. The recommendation is to master ordinary skills first: once a reliable method exists, moving it into Cowork and extending it with connectors or subagents becomes far easier.

Summary

In this chapter, we saw how connectors let Claude read from and, where supported, write to external tools. MCP provides the common standard, while connectors package that access for easier installation. The five-level model helps you choose the most efficient available route, and skills turn that access into repeatable processes such as proofreading Canva decks, reconciling Stripe data, and drafting follow-up emails from call recordings.

We then examined subagents as Cowork's way of delegating repeated or context-heavy work into separate contexts. Skills define the method, while subagents perform assigned parts of the work and return their results to the main conversation. They are most useful for heavy or parallel workloads, have no persistent identity, cannot create further subagents, and require Cowork. Connectors and subagents extend skills, but ordinary skills remain the foundation.

6

Unlock the Sample Skill Bundle and the PDF Version

Your copy of this book includes the following exclusive benefits:

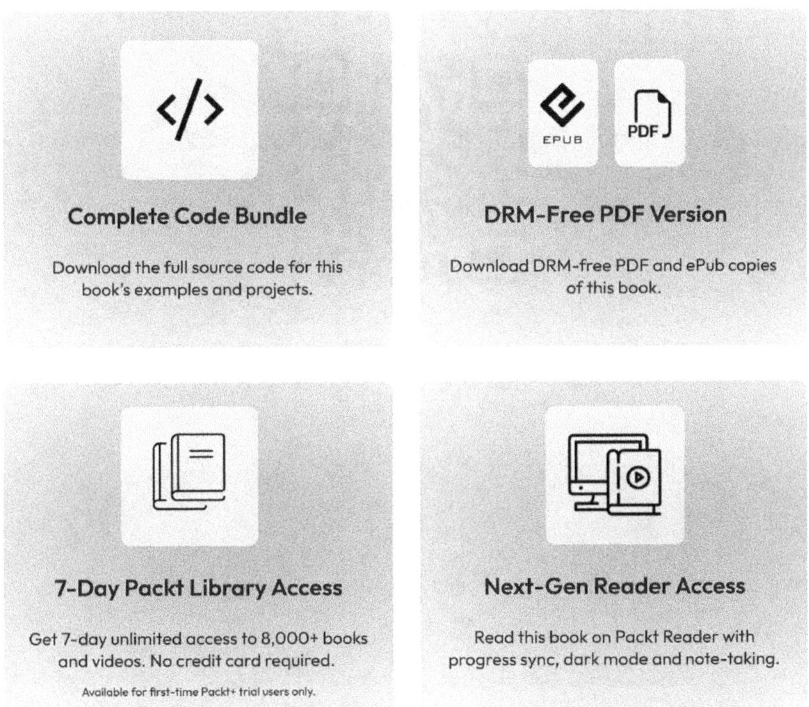

Follow this guide to unlock them. The process takes only a few minutes and only needs to be completed once.

Unlock this book's free benefits in three easy steps

Step 1

Have your purchase invoice ready for *step 3*. If you have a physical copy, scan it using your phone and save it as a PDF, JPG, or PNG.

For more help on finding your invoice, visit `https://www.packtpub.com/unlock-benefits/help`.

> NOTE
>
> **Note**: If you bought this book directly from the Packt website, no invoice is required. After *step 2*, you can access your exclusive content right away.

Step 2

Scan the QR code or go to `https://packtpub.com/unlock`.

On the page that opens (similar to *Figure 6.1* on desktop), search for this book by name and select the correct edition.

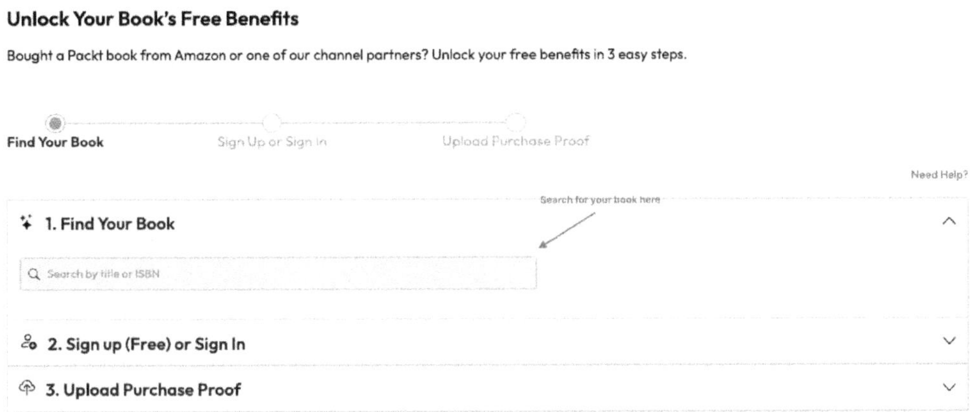

Figure 6.1: Packt unlock landing page on desktop

Step 3

After selecting the book, sign in to your Packt account or create one for free. Then, upload your invoice (PDF, PNG, or JPG, up to 10 MB). Follow the on-screen instructions to finish the process.

Need help?

If you get stuck and need help, visit `https://www.packtpub.com/unlock-benefits/help` for a detailed FAQ on how to find your invoice and more. This QR code will take you to the help page.

> NOTE
>
> **Note**: If you are still facing issues, reach out to `customercare@packt.com`.

Other Books You May Enjoy

If you enjoyed this book, you may be interested in these other books by Packt:

Everyone Is a Programmer

Zhang Bin, Wu Zhenyao

ISBN: 978-1-80730-559-8

- Confront the fears holding many beginners back
- Apply the Think, Prompt, Iterate philosophy
- Build apps with Cursor, Figma, v0.dev, and Supabase
- Turn natural language into professional UIs
- Use low-cost cloud services for scalable infrastructure
- Explore API design, database management, and MCP

Agentic Coding with Claude Code

Eden Marco

ISBN: 978-1-80602-259-5

- Design agentic coding workflows in the terminal and IDE using Claude Code
- Build custom automations with reusable slash commands and hooks
- Use Claude Code with a Next.js project to implement AI-driven workflows
- Create persistent AI memory using Claude Code memory files
- Apply MCP for structured context sharing across tools and agents
- Design multi-agent systems using subagents and orchestration patterns
- Enforce coding standards using project documentation and context control
- Scale AI pair programming while keeping code maintainable

Packt is searching for authors like you

If you're interested in becoming an author for Packt, please visit `authors.packt.com` and apply today. We have worked with thousands of developers and tech professionals, just like you, to help them share their insight with the global tech community. You can make a general application, apply for a specific hot topic that we are recruiting an author for, or submit your own idea.

Share your thoughts

Now you've finished *Building Claude Skills*, we'd love to hear your thoughts! Scan the QR code below to go straight to the Amazon review page for this book and share your feedback or leave a review on the site that you purchased it from.

`https://packt.link/r/1808492854`

Your review is important to us and the tech community and will help us make sure we're delivering excellent quality content.

Index

T

W

www.ingramcontent.com/pod-product-compliance
Lightning Source LLC
LaVergne TN
LVHW060043210926
848481LV00013B/3941
9781808492853